ADRIENNE RYAN

A Silent Love

ADRIENNE RYAN was born in the United Kingdom and spent her childhood in Zambia and Belgium before returning to England. A former police officer and corporate recruitment consultant, she took a career break to have her two children, Elizabeth and Georgina, and another to complete an honors degree in politics and international relations. She moved to Australia in 1996 and became a citizen three years later. She now writes for a living and consults on television drama production, while also fulfilling public speaking engagements on a variety of topics, including the emotional impact of miscarriage. *A Silent Love* is her first book, and a percentage of her royalties for it will go to the Newborn Intensive Care Center, Royal Hospital for Women, Sydney, Australia.

A Silent Love

A Silent Love

ADRIENNE RYAN

MARLOWE & COMPANY
NEW YORK

Published by
Marlowe & Company
An Imprint of Avalon Publishing Group Incorporated
161 William Street, 16th Floor
New York, NY 10038

First published by Penguin Books Australia 2000.
This edition published by arrangement.

LIBRARY OF CONGRESS CATALOGING-IN-PUBLICATION DATA
Ryan, Adrienne.
A silent love : personal stories of coming to terms with miscarriages / by
Adrienne Ryan.
p. cm.
Includes bibliographical references.
ISBN 1-56924-543-6
1. Miscarriage. 2. Miscarriage—Psychological aspect—Case studies. 3. Infants
(Newborn)—Death—Case studies. 4. Bereavement—Psychological aspects—
Case studies. I. Title.

RG648 .R93 2001
618.3'92—dc21   2001026624

9 8 7 6 5 4 3 2 1

Designed by Pauline Neuwirth, Neuwirth & Associates, Inc.

Printed in the United States of America
Distributed by Publishers Group West

To the memory of Simon and Clare Ryan,

born and died 17 April 1987:

our darling little children,

remembered with all the love you never knew.

To everything there is a season,

And a time to every purpose under heaven:

A time to be born, and a time to die...

Ecclesiastes 3: 1-2

Contents

Contents

Introduction

MOST YOUNG GIRLS GROW UP, AS I DID, WITH the belief that one day they'll be mothers. This belief may be conscious or unconscious, yearned for or simply tolerated, but, for the vast majority, once puberty kicks in, we are reminded of that biological possibility with regular monotony.

For me, motherhood was as much a given as the fact that one day I'd get married and in the fullness of time I'd grow old—provided, of course, that the fullness of time was slow! With maturity and hindsight, I now see that the only given is that there are simply no guarantees in this life. It is with frightening regularity that I meet excited young women who, seeing motherhood almost as a right, plan ahead as to which month and year their first child will be born. To point out that very often things don't go exactly according to plan can achieve little, as the adage "It will never happen to me" comes into play. The awful truth is that these plans can and do go wrong sometimes.

My husband Peter and I have endured several miscarriages over the past thirteen years and have come to realize just how common miscarriage actually is and how difficult it can be to come to terms with such a loss. My first pregnancy ended in a miscarriage at only eight weeks. The pregnancy had been unplanned, but, nevertheless, the sense of loss and feelings of guilt, anger, frustration, and hopelessness were enormous, and the loss suddenly brought with it a new meaning to my life. This totally unexpected cruel blow of fate left me with an emptiness that only another child could fill.

We agreed that I would try to get pregnant again as soon as possible, but getting pregnant, I soon learned, was not the problem for me; holding on to those precious babies was the difficulty I was to face in all my pregnancies.

When our twins, Simon and Clare, were born fifteen weeks prematurely, they had little chance of survival. Until a few years ago, a baby born before twenty-eight weeks' gestation was technically deemed to be a miscarriage. (See the glossary of medical terms for current definitions.) The twins' viability—the chance of their surviving to lead happy, healthy lives—was minimal, and consequently the medics were not inclined to make any attempt to keep them alive. Our twins lay quietly in incubators and within a few hours had both lost their short battles for life. The promise of a future we had been carrying with us as they grew inside me was wiped away in an instant, leaving only the miserable prospect of a very lonely funeral service.

When a baby dies, whether it is in the early or late stages of a pregnancy, at birth, or shortly after birth, we are left to cope with a multitude of emotions, all of which threaten to engulf us in grief. The emotional distress is compounded by the fact that there is often a lack of understanding by those around us, an almost incomprehensible questioning as to why, when we never knew our child, we should be feeling the overwhelming sense of loss we do.

The loss of a child is one of life's greatest tragedies. With one Australian study putting the rate of miscarriage as high as one in two, many women don't even realize they're pregnant at the time they miscarry. It is an all too frequent tragedy and one that is too infrequently discussed.* We need to allow ourselves—and we need to be allowed—to grieve openly, because this is no less than we deserve. The process of grieving is like a journey we must embark on in our search for answers as to why our babies died. The search requires that we reach a point where we as individuals can talk freely and honestly with others without feeling angry, guilty, or ashamed. This is a point that, as a society, we have not yet reached. Consequently an aura of taboo remains, and countless men and women have left their journeys incomplete.

---

* See Michael J. Bennett and D. Keith Edmonds, eds., *Spontaneous and Recurrent Abortion* (Melbourne: Blackwell Scientific Publications, 1987), which notes that figures for early embryonic loss vary from 25 percent (French and Bierman, 1962) to 78 percent (Roberts and Lowe, 1975). The only controlled study (Edmonds, et al., 1982), showed the figure to be around 50 percent. That study spanned the period from before conception and found that, of the pregnancies that were lost, over 90 percent occurred without the woman's knowledge.

It was this fact, more than any other, that left me with a burning need to make a change and do something for others who have experienced the death of a child in this way. I've long held the belief that with enough strength, desire, and determination, I could create some good from my personal experiences of miscarriage. Of course, wanting to do something and actually doing it are two very different things. I frequently thought about writing this book, but the time was never right. Looking back now that I have finally completed what I set out to do, I realize why that was: I still harbored so much hurt and so much anger at the apparent injustice of it all. Deep down I must have known that the process of revisiting my own grief and sharing the grief and pain of others would have an extremely profound effect on me, and I was frightened by that prospect.

Then I made the "mistake" of speaking publicly about my last miscarriage, and suddenly I found myself being criticized in a newspaper for openly discussing a subject that should "be kept within the confines of the home." I was incensed. It was exactly this sort of comment that encouraged and nurtured the taboo against miscarriage and stillbirth, exactly the sort of comment that encouraged women to feel ashamed or guilty about what is, in fact, a tragedy. With a renewed determination, I told myself that I would not allow such ignorance to make me ashamed of who or what I am. It was therefore anger of a very different sort that finally gave me the impetus to follow through with my dream.

I felt strongly that the book should reflect the fact that miscarriage, stillbirth, and neonatal death are such frequent occurrences. I didn't want to write exclusively about my own experiences, thoughts, and beliefs, but to seek out other men and women who would be prepared to share their heartbreak. To that end I am grateful to the journalists I spoke to at the *Sun Herald* newspaper and *Woman's Day* magazine for the help they gave me in finding those people. Each of the two publications wrote about the project I was embarking on and asked people to write to me, and we were all amazed at the huge response the articles elicited from around the country. Several replies even arrived from other countries, from men and women whose friends or family members had passed on the information. Hundreds upon hundreds of letters poured in by mail, and a great many other stories came from a request placed on the Internet and from people I spoke to in England. The response was truly international, and as I sorted through the replies, the reality hit me: I had now made a commitment to others. It was no longer just me I would be letting down if I failed to complete what I had set out to do.

Writing this book has proved to be an extraordinarily important part of my own journey of grief and discovery. There have been many, many times over the past thirteen years when I have sat down with friends and recounted the details of my experience. I tried to explain why I harbor such a deep sense of loss and why I still grieve, but on each occasion I failed. I was, I believe, incapable of reasoning my own thoughts and understanding my own feelings, so how could I possibly have expressed them adequately to others?

Then I found that researching the topic, although very sad, became an incredibly enlightening period of my life, during which I finally reached an understanding of my own grief and therefore the grief of others. We need to understand why the emotional impact of this tragedy is so often all-consuming in order to fully grieve the death of our child. We need to understand why our grief is unique.

Not only was writing this book a difficult process for me, but it also had a profound impact on my husband. Initially he had no desire to open his wounds and share his side of our story. Instead, he wanted simply to support me emotionally when the going got tough, as he knew it would, and when I became moody and difficult as I struggled with trying to come to terms, yet again, with what had happened to us. It was when he agreed to read the draft manuscript that his attitude changed, and he decided he would like to tell his story after all. He understood what I was trying to achieve and he wanted to contribute to that. We have rarely discussed our losses with each other, dealing with our grief in our own way, as many couples do, so when I read his words, I glimpsed a less familiar part of the man I married, and I love him all the more for finding the strength to share that with others.

I hope that this book will achieve two things: first, that by sharing the experiences of others and gaining an understanding of their emotions, it will give support and hope to men and women who have suffered this tragedy recently or in the distant past and second, that it will give our families and friends an explanation of the unique elements of grief that surround our loss. Hopefully, they'll then understand how important it is to acknowledge not only that our child existed in the first place, but also the important part they can play by loving and supporting those couples trying to come to terms with the death of a child.

Understanding Our Grief

A CHILD CREATED THROUGH THE LOVE OF TWO adults is indeed a precious gift. From the moment of conception, each of our babies offers us a potential for the future—a potential for our future, promising fundamental changes to our lives that, while in many ways unimaginable, are also absolutely imagined and extraordinary. For the majority of prospective parents, that potential is realized when their child is born and grows to become an essential member of their family: a child, an adolescent, and ultimately an adult who contributes much to the richness of the lives he or she touches each day.

But for others, sadly, the potential is never realized, and a future is lost. So far-reaching are the implications of that loss that it cannot be dealt with as an isolated incident, but this is usually what we try to do and, moreover, what others expect us to do. Yet the loss remains an intrinsic part of our lives, the ramifications of which reverberate ever after.

With each day and with each event the surviving family members enjoy, there remains a constant vacuum, a space that was reserved for a child to fill or at least partly fill. We remain constantly aware that, while our child would have said and done many things to alter our lives, our lives are instead altered by all the things that child hasn't said and done. It is our future that has been affected, not our past. When a parent or other relative who has been a part of our past dies, we have tangible memories of that person and of the contribution he or she made to our lives. If we have happy times to remember, for the most part we can ultimately come to an acceptance of his or her death. But when a baby dies, no memories exist to help us reach such an acceptance. We are not able to look back and remember things about our own child that might make us smile, and it is this fact that is fundamental to the explanation of our grief and that makes it a grief unlike any other.

Men and women grieve in very different ways. For the mother, the impact of miscarriage or stillbirth is both physical and emotional. While the death of a friend or a family member is in itself devastating, the death of a baby who hasn't yet lived outside the womb constitutes the loss of part of herself. When a baby who is still a physical part of our own body dies, an actual part of us dies too, and the grief is therefore twofold.

Furthermore, when a baby dies at a time when its dependency on the mother is absolute, many women subsequently feel that they have failed their child and failed in their most basic function of womanhood. The feelings of guilt and failure can often be so intense that they risk falling into an abyss of self-doubt from which some become incapable of returning.

Throughout a pregnancy, the identity of the woman begins to slowly and inextricably alter. We begin to change in the eyes of those around us, from simply being an individual to being a prospective mother. Whether it is to be our first child or our fifth, our identity is going to change, and our life choices begin to change accordingly. When our baby dies during the pregnancy or soon afterwards, the new identity that has been built for us dies as well. It is a sudden, cruel, heart-wrenching, and very lonely ending, and to begin again we need a great deal of help.

Unfortunately, in order to get the help we so desperately need, we actually have to be open to receiving it, and often we just aren't. Where others expect us to go out and actively seek that help, we are in fact emotionally incapable of doing so. The anger and hurt can manifest itself in ways we don't recognize as a part of our usual character, and consequently we close ourselves off from those we need the most. It is not unusual, for example, to try and lay blame on those around us—husband, partners, parents, medical professionals, anyone who has been involved with us during the pregnancy.

Similarly, it is not unusual to feel jealous and resentful toward—or even to avoid seeing—friends and family members who are enjoying healthy pregnancies or who already have young children and seem oblivious to the pain we are experiencing. The desperate need for others to understand what we are going through has many women wishing the same tragedy upon others. It is not that we wish others sadness, it is simply that sometimes we believe this is the only way they will ever understand the emotional and physical impact of our loss.

These kinds of feelings bring with them the added emotion of shame, but the truth is that having these feelings is quite natural during what is an otherwise unnaturally traumatic period. Sadly, though, because some mothers can feel so alone in their grief and fail to realize this, they unwittingly create a barrier around themselves, thus compounding the loneliness.

For the father, the impact of miscarriage or stillbirth is primarily emotional, but physical in the sense that he is traditionally expected to remain strong for his partner and must therefore suppress the natural grieving process. He must come to terms with his own grief as well as, in most cases, the grief of his partner. To the outside world he must show strength of character, leaving little room for tears, because this is how society tells him he must behave. He is expected to sacrifice his own emotions for the sake of the woman, as her grief, although too little understood by others, is at least better understood than his own. People, mothers included, generally do not acknowledge the fact that while he was not the one who physically nurtured the unborn child, the child was his nonetheless. He too has nurtured ideas of a future as a father and he too must feel free to grieve.

Unfortunately, our society being the way it is, whichever way a man chooses to grieve, he can find himself in a no-win situation. Openly grieving can leave him a subject for ridicule by his friends—although by the same token, of course, those women who appreciate his sensitivity will admire him. Those who succumb to the traditional "male" method of internalizing their pain and moving on with their lives, seemingly unaffected by the tragedy, often then face the hurt of their partner, who cannot comprehend their attitude. This kind of misunderstanding can put an enormous strain on a relationship and is further complicated when the partners, who are physically and emotionally drained from their horrendous experience, find communication difficult. The impact of the loss of a child on the relationship between the parents is therefore another unique factor of this grief. A mother who feels she is to blame may fear her partner believes the same; seeing herself as a failure, she may believe he sees her that way too. If she has created a barrier between herself and others, she might then also create a barrier between herself and her partner.

Couples need to feel able to talk to each other as well as to others. An appreciation of each other's differences when it comes to dealing with grief is as important as an appreciation by others of their combined grief. An understanding by everyone involved of the whys and wherefores surrounding the grief of miscarriage, stillbirth, and neonatal death is paramount. If we as parents can understand why this multitude of emotions is threatening to engulf us and that our shame and guilt are a part of human nature, then we will more willingly embrace offers of help. If those around us understand why we grieve the way we do, then they in turn will be more willing and more able to offer that essential love, support, and care, and thus empower us in the healing process.

The greatest gift anyone can give grieving parents is the gift of understanding. And there is another great gift, the gift of acknowledgement—the acknowledgement that we had a child who died and that we have lost the potential of a life that, for us, held the promise of something quite extraordinary, the acknowledgement that our lives will never be the same again.

MY STORY

I MARRIED at the age of twenty-four with the thought of children not uppermost in my mind. I was in love: here was a man who loved me, someone I could talk, laugh, and make love with, and who was my best friend. All our hopes, dreams, and aspirations would come into being when the time was right, and children, if we chose to have them, would come along because that was my right. I had yet to learn, through the loss of my precious babies, that to have a child is actually not a right but a privilege.

By the time Peter and I had been married eighteen months, I had already been taking the contraceptive pill for several years. The frequent stories in the press about the detrimental side effects of hormonal contraception, compounded by the fact that I was a smoker, helped me decide to come off the pill and go in search of an alternative. I chose the cap, and I'm sure that the success of this form of contraception is in no small measure due to the problematic way women are expected to prepare and insert it. Spontaneity flies rapidly out the window and, equally rapidly, fatigue sets in during the search for the elusive slippery object, which has typically lodged itself in some seldom explored corner of the bathroom!

Needless to say, due rather more to carelessness than to design, it didn't take long before I found myself pregnant. How many accidental pregnancies are just that? I wonder, because I can't, with absolute certainty, say there wasn't some part of me that was yearning for a child, and I've no doubt my subconscious has lied to me over the years. Suffice it to say I was pregnant, and for the first time in my life there was another human being whose physical and mental development was totally and utterly dependent on me.

For Peter, there was the pride he felt at fathering a child and the knowledge that this little person, whom we had created together, would arrive into this world bringing for us a responsibility like no other: the responsibility to nurture this child and help him or her grow physically, emotionally, and intellectually. Planned or not, we were delighted at the prospect of becoming parents, but as the enormity of the situation began to sink in, a wave of new emotions swept over us, and with it came feelings of absolute terror. Sadly, though, in the eighth week of pregnancy I started to bleed, and all of those feelings rapidly changed to trepidation.

A threatened miscarriage during the early stages of a pregnancy generally prompts the medical profession to suggest you take a period of what they term bed rest. In moments of honesty, however, they acknowledge that resting can do little to sustain a pregnancy; it merely offers comfort to the couple, who may then feel something tangible and constructive is being done. If the baby is lost, one can console oneself with the knowledge that this happened despite one's best efforts. Essentially, though, the treatment is a placebo.

Being young and naive about pregnancy, I hung on every word the professionals threw at me and lay, as directed, in a ward with thirty other women. On my side of the room were two women who, like me, were trying desperately to hold on to that tiny piece of humanity they held in their wombs. On the other side were four very young women who had undergone voluntary terminations of their pregnancies. I don't condemn those women for exercising their right to choose, but to this day I'm hurt and bewildered by the logic of the medical staff who placed us all together. I can vaguely recall a comment made by one of the nursing staff that indicated they were keen to have women like me on display in an effort to heighten the feelings of guilt for those girls who were there for their second, third, or even fourth abortions. It is the horror of that memory that I think today prevents me from regaining total clarity. I wonder if at any time consideration was given to the effect such action had on those of us who had no choice whatsoever in whether our babies lived or died.

During a miscarriage and for a short while afterwards, pregnancy hormones remain in a woman's system. Hospital staff look for signs of a viable pregnancy by testing whether there is a stability in or gradual reduction of these hormone levels. During my few days in the hospital, I had numerous pregnancy tests and ultrasound scans, but as the days progressed my hopes for this baby gradually died.

Each morning I would wake up and pray for feelings of nausea to sweep over me. The one ray of hope the nurses had given was that morning sickness was the strongest sign of a healthy pregnancy. I knew, as I went through the charade of turning down the cooked breakfast and asking instead for a plain biscuit, that my apparent queasiness was actually only a symptom of my mental desperation. There was a vast difference between my feelings and those of the woman in the bed next to me, who was genuinely sick, genuinely blue, and genuinely still pregnant. Seven months later she sent me a birth announcement saying she had

had a healthy baby boy whom she named James. I never saw her again.

I left the hospital to all intents and purposes no different physically from the way I'd been eight weeks before, but my life had taken on a new perspective. Something fundamental to my existence had been taken away from me, and I found myself incapable of moving on without resolution. Getting pregnant again became my goal to the exclusion of all else and, despite the doctor's suggestion that we wait, two months later I was pregnant once more. It was quickly established that this time I was carrying twins.

After a miscarriage, the words "Don't worry, you can always have another one" are frequently bandied about by those who cannot comprehend the enormity of the loss. The child who has gone can never be replaced: that child's individuality, character, physical features, values, and beliefs would have been his or hers alone and can never be transposed onto any subsequent child. For me, the fact that I was now carrying twins did not make up for the child we'd lost, but it did feel a little like we were being blessed with winning the lottery and the bonus prize.

When I look back, one of the most striking things about that pregnancy was my ability to know and understand my body, despite the hormonal changes I'd never previously experienced. A woman will normally begin to experience a tightening of the uterus at around thirty-six weeks; mine began at twelve weeks. I'd read enough to know that the purpose of these practice contractions was to prepare the womb to expel the baby, and as it was still so soon after losing my first baby, I couldn't rid myself of the fear of losing the children I was now carrying. Countless times I

wept on the phone to my mother, telling her that I just knew
something wasn't right. Countless times I wept to my obstetrician, reiterating those same fears, only to be met by condescend-
ing remarks implying I knew nothing and he knew everything.

Twenty weeks into the pregnancy, I became so distressed that
my doctor agreed to put me in the hospital for closer examination. A senior midwife—a total dragon who was unmarried, with
no personal experience of pregnancy—was told to monitor my
contractions. She spent a long time hooking me up to various
monitors, and over the next few hours several of the contractions
registered clearly on the printouts. Later that evening, before my
doctor came back for the results, she tore those results up and
then told him there had been nothing to see. It was another
example, for me, of a tendency on the part of the medical profession to assume their learned knowledge tells them more than the
innate knowledge of their patients. It was also another example
of my own tendency to rely, without question, on the experts.

Many of the friends I speak to about having children talk
about the almost complete loss of inhibition that comes with the
constant scrutiny women are subjected to during a pregnancy. It
appears to be a requisite of this condition that we get used to
lying with our legs in the air under the ever closer examination
of doctors. Worse, if one happens to be in a training hospital,
there can be as many as ten nervous interns present, each of
whom, while looking intelligently into those most intimate of
places, is trying desperately not to make eye contact with the
owner. It seemed that my obstetrician had a penchant for carrying out these internal examinations. When I was twenty-five
weeks pregnant, he again examined me and found that I was

dilating. He was a man with an inordinate amount of experience, but nevertheless, with an ignorance he had no right to have, he sent me home with instructions to admit myself the next day.

I lay in bed that night becoming increasingly aware of the tightening in my womb, until at 4:30 A.M. I asked Peter to take me to the hospital. My sleepy obstetrician examined me again, but this time he explained I'd now dilated to such an extent that there was no longer anything he could do for me. My babies would have to be born and, undoubtedly, they would die.

One of the problems with a twin birth is that twice as many doctors, nurses, and cribs must be catered. The twin delivery suite at the hospital in the town where we were living did not have a twin delivery room, so I found myself being whisked into an ambulance and eventually taken to a nearby city. Unfortunately, the ambulance driver had never been to that hospital and was forced to ring the local police for directions. At 6:00 A.M. they were relatively underemployed and came out in their droves not only to escort the ambulance, but also to stop traffic at each junction, enabling us to pass through red lights.

That journey provided us with some much-needed light relief. Halfway to the hospital we realized that Peter, who was following at speed in his own car, had been stopped by a young police officer. The policeman had understandably made the assumption that my husband was tailing the ambulance purely to get to work faster, and despite what we knew lay ahead for us, we were able to laugh.

When faced with a highly traumatic situation, people will often do and say things that appear totally inappropriate but that help maintain some order of sanity. For us this interlude offered only a very brief respite. As we waited in the delivery suite, a young doctor walked in and said, "They do know they're going to die, don't they?"

Five hours later I gave birth to a little boy and a little girl. After the babies were born, they were moved to another room and placed in separate incubators. The incubators were not operating for life support, however, because at that time there was a general belief that to keep babies of twenty-five weeks' gestation alive required substantial amounts of oxygen, which in turn often led to severe physical and mental abnormalities. It was a question of quality of life, and in the case of my babies none could be guaranteed. They were tiny and they were perfect, but just too tiny to survive. This was to be the last time in my life that I was prepared to accept the word of someone in the medical profession without question. With no experience of their own, they meant well, but for the rest of my life, the fact that I followed their instructions to return to my room and leave my babies will remain my greatest regret. I did as I was told, and because of that my babies died alone.

After it was all over, Peter was told to return home. I was left alone and placed in a maternity ward where all the other mothers were nursing their newborn children. I cannot begin to put into words the pain I experienced sitting there with them as their babies cried and they asked me what I'd had. I left that hospital within hours of having given birth, and I returned to my home with a shattering sense of loss and hopelessness.

Throughout the labor, and afterwards, we were joined by a young priest named Michael who sat and prayed with us, christening the babies before they died. His patience and understanding were remarkable for one who had never before experienced this type of tragedy. Later, his wisdom helped us to reach a decision about the funeral arrangements, and we were able to allevi-ate some of our overwhelming feelings of guilt by laying the babies together in one very small white coffin. They will now never be lonely in death, as they had been in life.

Simon and Clare were born on Good Friday, 1987. On Easter Sunday Peter and I went to church, but I found that within a few minutes I had to leave. I believed I was a good person, I had never set out to do harm to anyone, and yet here I was with the most unbearable hurt, and for the life of me I could not find any way to understand how God could have let this happen to me. To this day I retain a theoretical belief in God, but the strength of that belief has undoubtedly lessened. Even now I can remem-ber clearly the days that followed during which I sat alone in my garden, mentally beating myself with all the questions of guilt that most women in my situation must contend with. Knowing how self-destructive my actions were, I returned to work imme-diately, and for the first time I became aware of how difficult most people find it to cope with another's loss and grief. Their lack of understanding renders them incapable of anything other than the occasional banal platitude. They genuinely want to help, but they can't know that what you need is to be hugged and, more important, that you desperately need them to understand how acute your loss is, regardless of how soon the pregnancy has ended.

This lack of understanding and awareness results in a need for the couple who has been through the tragedy to rely heavily on each other. During the time Peter and I were enduring the mis-carriages, neither of us knew anyone who had been through a similar experience to whom we could turn for support and advice.

We had each other, but, being individuals, we each dealt with our grief in different ways.

It can be easy for the woman, who for a while retains many physical reminders of the child, to forget that her emotional loss is equalled by that of her partner. I'd like to believe I wasn't like that, that I was as much there for Peter as he was for me, but I don't know. Where I have a tendency to externalize my emotions, he will internalize his, and he is therefore more able to compartmentalize events in his life and move on to the next task. When it came to the loss of our babies, this next task was to give strength to me and to see me through a time when I believed myself to be a failure in the most basic function of womanhood.

Three months later I was pregnant again, and in 1988, having spent several months in the hospital, during which time my cervix was stitched and I took four-hourly doses of a muscle-relaxant drug, I gave birth to Elizabeth. She was four weeks early and a healthy weight, but as Peter watched over her he became aware that something was wrong with her breathing. Within minutes she was whisked away to the special care unit, where she remained for three weeks, attached to every conceivable piece of medical machinery. It was not until the day before we took her home that the nurses and doctors would give us any indication of how they rated her chances of survival. Before that, we were left to wonder whether or not yet another of our darling children would be taken from us. The following year Georgina arrived. She too was four weeks early, but fortunately did not go through the same difficulties as her sister's.

Today, to all intents and purposes, we are a typical, loving family, but underlying that happiness for me is the knowledge that over the past thirteen years I have never allowed myself the luxury of finalizing my grief. Rather than completing that journey in order to be able to move forward as an entirely whole individual again, I have jumped in and out of it. There have been so many changes in my life, most particularly the frequent moves that have come about as a result of my husband's career, that there has rarely been a time of stability and peace suited to completing my journey. As a result, all the repressed feelings of guilt, grief, and even anger tend to come bubbling back to the surface of my consciousness, often triggered by totally unconnected and relatively unimportant events.

Peter and I consider ourselves lucky now to have two beautiful, healthy, bright young daughters. I count myself lucky to have been able to get pregnant easily. There are countless people, I know, who spend months and years trying to conceive, often without success. We get so much pleasure watching our children grow. We are constantly amazed at how their individuality is expressed through what they say and what they do. As they reach for and overcome life's many hurdles, we sit back smiling and wait for what comes next. But through it all, not a day goes by when we don't think of the children we've lost and wonder at what might have been, at who they would have become and what they might have been capable of achieving.

PETER'S STORY

I REMEMBER the first time: I was away on business when I received a call from my father-in-law telling me Adrienne had been admitted to the hospital with all the symptoms of an impending miscarriage. As I drove to the hospital, a wave of emotions swept over me. Was I a father? Did I want to be a father? We hadn't ever seriously discussed the possibility of children, but now I was overcome by an inexplicable sense of loss at what might have been after all, a feeling that was amplified when I arrived at the hospital and the miscarriage was confirmed by Adrienne's drawn features and tearful story.

Within a couple of months, she became pregnant again, a pregnancy this time planned for and anticipated. To make sure she had the best of care, we decided to seek private treatment from the obstetrician, and on our first visit to him we discovered we were expecting twins. We were excited, amazed, and overjoyed. Twins seemed to be a huge bonus.

Adrienne made frequent visits to the doctor and had numerous tests and what appeared to be the best of care, but after one particular visit she came home upset. She was convinced there was something wrong, but the doctor thought she was being overanxious. I tried to reassure her, and together we made all the usual arrangements in anticipation of the two small people who would be joining our home and family in a few months' time. Strollers, cribs, fabrics, toys, and color schemes were all chosen and discussed at length. We even exchanged our two-seater sports car for a station wagon and blocked off dates in our diaries. Emotionally and physically, we prepared ourselves for parenthood.

Unfortunately, Adrienne continued to have contractions and became increasingly concerned about the pregnancy. Visits to the doctor increased, and concern began to push expectancy to one side. After a second visit in as many days, this time to the maternity ward, I collected Adrienne to take her home. She was very upset because her cervix was dilating and she had been told to return to the hospital the next day for more treatment. Next day, next day! What about now? Why go home if things were looking serious? Why not more medication, anything? I asked all these questions, but we went home anyway, trusting in the advice from the experts.

Then, at 4:30 the next morning, Adrienne went into labor. She was just twenty-five weeks pregnant, and we both knew the awful possibilities. I rang the hospital to tell them we were on our way.

We drove off into the cold, dark April morning. It was foggy, visibility was poor, and the roads were icy. During the twelve-mile journey, Adrienne sat white with pain, saying, "Please be quick, Peter." When we finally arrived, the staff were waiting, a room was prepared, and we were told the doctor was on his way. We waited, and he arrived about fifteen minutes later. The concern on his face and on those of the nursing staff was all too apparent. It didn't look good.

After a quick examination, the doctor told us that the birth was imminent but that the hospital we were at didn't have the facilities for a premature twin delivery. We would have to go to Leeds, fifteen miles away, where suitable facilities existed. An ambulance was summoned and Adrienne stretchered on board. I was told to follow by car. "Where to?" I asked. "St. James," was the reply. The famous Jimmy's—I was relieved. This world-famous hospital had everything; they would be able to help, wouldn't they?

We set off, the ambulance first, with me trailing along behind. The fog had got worse and driving was slow, with frequent braking often bringing us almost to a standstill. Please hurry up, I pleaded. Please God, take away the fog, help my wife, save my children. I had no idea what was going on in the ambulance or how she was feeling, whether she was hurting or worrying.

Suddenly, we turned off the Leeds road. We started heading in a different direction, and the emergency blue and red lights started to flash on top of the ambulance. My heart nearly stopped. What was going on? What was happening in the ambulance? I wanted to shout out, Stop! For God's sake tell me. But of course no one would have heard me. The fog was still thick, and as we entered the outskirts of Bradford, I saw that the police were stopping traffic, and a police car with flashing blue lights had come to escort us. I felt helpless, alone, and incapable of doing anything for my wife, who was just a few yards in front of me and behind the white doors of the ambulance. Please let everything be all right, I said to myself.

It was still early when we drove up to the hospital, and very few people were about. I realized that the ambulance men were looking for the way in, an open door. Surely it's not closed, I thought. It was, but finally a side door opened and a nurse appeared and whisked Adrienne into the delivery room, where the nurses and doctors began to examine her. She looked terrified and awfully ill as the senior midwife told me there was nothing they could do to stop the babies arriving; Adrienne was just too far gone.

When I asked why we had not gone to Jimmy's, the answer was disturbing. Jimmy's was full, with no more room for premature babies. They couldn't handle any more, and apparently we were fortunate to have got into this hospital, as they didn't normally receive patients during the night. It was only because the ambulance crew made special pleas and declared an emergency that they had been allowed to come. "Where else could we have gone?" I asked. "I don't know," came the reply, "I'm sorry." No, this cannot possibly be England, I thought to myself.

I watched as my first child was born, and when I looked at him he was so perfectly formed. I was surprised that he was so big; I had expected a premature baby to be tiny. I remember thinking he looked just like me. The nurse took him away, hurrying off with the little bundle, small arms and legs moving and little mewing sounds coming from inside the blue blanket. As she left the room, I was told to press the button if we needed someone. Adrienne and I were alone.

I wanted to shout, Wait, there are twins. There's another one. Adrienne was crying. She was in pain and in shock and I felt helpless, hopeless, and useless, confined to holding her hand and stroking her hair. It seemed no sooner had the medical staff left the room than the labor started all over again. I saw the head of my second child appear and desperately tried to remember which button the nurse had told me to press. I called out and then turned to help Adrienne and the baby. Our little girl, when she arrived, was perfect and was almost completely delivered when the midwife and doctors finally pushed me out of the way. They took her away immediately.

Adrienne and I simply hugged and held each other, murmuring words of support and hopeless speculation that our children would survive, but it ended when we held our dying children in our arms as the priest administered the first and last rites. All of us—the priest, the nurses, Adrienne and I—wept over their little bodies. We wept for their lost lives and for all the things they would never see or know.

I couldn't help thinking, through all the numbness, that this was really a nightmare. Surely this amount of pain could not be real? What was God doing to let this happen?

Adrienne was exhausted, in a state of shock and now, thankfully, sedated. I was told to leave and to call later to arrange a time to collect her and take her home. After I left, the staff, in what seemed like an act of cruelty but in truth was simply a lack of thought, put Adrienne in a ward with women who had recently given birth to healthy, live babies.

I don't remember the long drive home or the telephoning of relatives and friends. I barely remember returning to the hospital that evening and bringing Adrienne home. I do, however, remember the doctor coming to see us the next day, and I remember how hard I found it to be civil. I blamed him for not keeping my wife in the hospital on her last visit, because if he had it might have saved the lives of my children. He didn't stay very long.

These days, twenty-five weeks offers a higher probability of survival for premature babies, but it was not so in 1987. As a husband, I had to be strong for my wife. People always asked how she was and whether she'd recovered. They didn't ask me how I was. Men have to appear emotionally strong at all times; I was brought up that way. At least now, because of my own experience, I can understand the emotional impact of miscarriage, and I have been able to offer support to friends suffering similar tragedies.

I often find myself wondering how the twins would have grown up, and now, being the father of two bright and beautiful daughters, I could weep, knowing that my firstborn children will never share in the love I have for them.

Our youngest daughter's middle name is Clare, after her sister. Clare and Simon will never be able to revel in the companionship of their sisters, and they will never experience their siblings' wide-eyed exploration of the world about them, and I will never know or understand the love a father has for his son.

Empty Arms

*I*T SEEMS A REASONABLE EXPECTATION FOR US ALL that when the love we have for another human being crystallizes itself in the conception of a child, it will be us, not our child, who will die first. For our child to die before us, and to die before even having had the opportunity to experience all that this world has to offer, is unthinkable.

Our friends and families want to empathize with us, but when they have not encountered a similar experience, whether their own or someone else's, they just can't. Most people are not equipped emotionally to place themselves in another person's trauma zone without having had that experience and are found wanting, inadequate in their ability to give help. As the grieving parents, we are then left not only to deal with our own feelings, but also to find a way to open ourselves enough to enable others to help us. It's a huge task all round, but it's a necessary task, as these others are the very people from whom we will ultimately draw some of the strength we need to see us through. If no other message is received from the stories in this book, let there at least be the realization that we have to help each other.

There can be no doubt that for many people a part of the strength they need to move on after the death of their child comes from their deep sense of faith, a belief in God and his love. But having faith in the first place can also present an additional burden for some. The feelings of anger many parents encounter after the death of their baby can result, quite naturally, in a questioning of their faith, no matter how strong it may be. All that has been learned may be challenged through the sheer frustration at how unfair life is, and we start to ask how or why God could allow us to suffer the way we are.

I was brought up by a Catholic mother and an Anglican father. My mother, who had been raised in a fairly strict regime of Catholicism, would take my sisters and me to church every Sunday; my father would join us for the occasional high day and holiday service. Despite the fact that I also attended Catholic schools, I don't remember ever feeling any great intensity of faith. I certainly believed in God, I believed in the concept of Christianity, but going to church was something I did because I felt I ought to, rather than because I felt I needed or wanted to. As an adult, my attendance at church lapsed, but my basic faith remained. I lived in a way I believed was good, honest, and decent.

I cannot remember a time when I deliberately did or said anything to cause pain or harm to another human being—I was a regular young woman, leading a regular, uneventful life.

When Peter and I married, we made the decision that we would start to go to church together, and most Sundays we did. Then I gave birth to my first children and for some inexplicable and totally unacceptable reason they died. When I walked out of church two days later, I couldn't stop the tears, and I've never been back. Have I lost my faith? I really can't answer that question, apart from saying I don't think so. But I know I have lost some essential part of what was fundamental to any conviction I had before my babies died.

It is my personal belief that when we search for answers, it is quite reasonable for some of us to question God. Doing so can be an extremely frightening experience, but it's important that as individuals we allow ourselves to undergo the process of reexamining our faith without adding to the guilt we already feel about what has happened. No one can guarantee what the outcome of that reexamination will be, but where faith has been strong, most people will ultimately find a new level of strength, purpose, and belief in their lives. For some of the women who share their stories in this chapter, God provided the inner strength by which they were able to continue.

Sharron's Story

Though I am now the proud mother of four healthy children, I will always remain the mother of a baby son, William, who was stillborn in 1985. My baby died because of a sudden antepartum hemorrhage that was not detectable at the time and that could not have been treated with medical intervention.

The actual delivery of my baby was a physical nightmare, because it had to be artificially induced and managed. Although it was done very professionally and with great compassion, it amounted to twenty hours of hell and left me weak with exhaustion and blood loss. At the time I just wanted to die, because I simply couldn't see how I could live with what had happened. For the next few months, the only goal in my life was to get pregnant again, and eventually I succeeded. I was thrilled and nervous, but unfortunately, just before Christmas, I was rushed to the hospital for emergency surgery, as they'd discovered I had an ectopic pregnancy. Strangely, after the operation I still felt pregnant, so I demanded they do a pregnancy test. To everyone's amazement, the result was positive; I had been expecting twins! One baby had been ectopic, but the other, thank God, had been intrauterine. I immediately named her Bridget, in the certain belief that she would be a girl.

The pregnancy was long and tough. I became quite depressed, because I could not accept that I had not done something that caused the death of my first baby. I was obsessed with the notion that the hemorrhage in the first pregnancy had happened because I had reached up to shut a high window the night before. For a long time, despite all the people who tried to convince me otherwise, including friends and medical experts, I clung to this illogical and self-damaging idea. Then it finally occurred to me that if any of my friends or my sister had lost their baby I would be sympathetic and not hold them accountable for what had happened. It was at that point, which was five years later, that I began the process of forgiving myself for losing my child.

I carry my son's memory always, and I still remember so clearly the image of his tiny face as my husband cradled him in his arms. I never held him and I wish I had, but at the time I was so distressed I didn't know that it might have been a good thing to do. All I have now is a photo, but it is indistinct, and unfortunately his little face had been injured during delivery.

We scattered his ashes in a lovely place in the Hunter Valley where we had also scattered the ashes of my sister-in-law, who'd died two years earlier from cystic fibrosis. Later I wished we'd buried him, but I've come to terms with the fact that what we did was right at the time. Every year on his birthday, I buy flowers for baby William, and I make sure I tell the florists who they are for so that they create something special. Every year we also remember Bridget's twin and how fortunate we are to have her with us.

I have since had three more children—Rhiannon and twins Rebecca and Brendan—but the grief of my first loss has never left me. It's hard to find positives from such tragedy, but I have salvaged anything I could from those experiences. First, I was very prepared for motherhood, and I really threw myself into it, gaining pleasure from it, and second, I became a more compassionate person and better able to be a friend to others who experience sorrow.

LYN'S STORY

PUTTING THIS into words is very difficult for me; even though it has been nine years since it happened, I feel as though it was only yesterday. Not many people seem to understand, so it's sometimes difficult to talk to anyone about it. Somehow it's as if they just don't want to know. Two days before Christmas in 1989, we discovered we were expecting twins. For the first twenty-four hours we were in shock, because we already had a twenty-one-month-old daughter, but then the joy of the situation overtook us. We began to think that our family would be complete, as we'd already decided that three was our magical number.

Then, two months later, everything seemed to go wrong; I started to swell up like a balloon, which I thought was probably normal for someone expecting twins, but then I started to bleed. I immediately called my obstetrician, who took me straight into the hospital, and by that evening I was hooked up to every kind of machine you can imagine.

For three days they did all they could to try to stop the contractions that by then had set in, but it was all to no avail. On February 14th, Valentine's Day and our third wedding anniversary, I gave birth to our twin girls, Lauren Anne and Nicole Louise. I was only twenty-three weeks pregnant, and unfortunately I had to have an emergency cesarean, so when they were born I was under a general anesthetic. I never got to see them while they were alive, but I thank God that my husband and our priest were there for the birth and were able to baptize the girls before they died. They lived for only ten minutes, and they died in my husband's arms.

When I think back to that day, it is like a dream, and I wonder how I ever got through it. My husband, Michael, was great at the time, and he still is. If we thought we were close before it happened, it astounds us just how much closer we felt during that period in our lives. We were told that one in every thousand twin pregnancies ends in miscarriage, and I must have asked myself a thousand times, Where are the other nine hundred and ninety-nine, and why should they have healthy babies? I am not a bad person, and I simply couldn't understand why this was happening to me.

My husband is also a very good and loving man, and he is a good father to our children, but people treated him as though his feelings of grief were unimportant. He was hurting terribly, but when people offered their condolences, they were only offering them to me, forgetting him completely. I don't think they did it to hurt him, it was just that it didn't occur to them to speak to him as well. I suppose they thought that, being a man, he wouldn't feel the pain as much as I did, but how wrong they were.

Since then we have had another two beautiful little girls, and life goes on, or so they tell me. It does go on, but for us something is missing. I tell my girls that we are in fact a family of seven, but two of ours are in Heaven. Of course they don't understand yet, but one day, when they're older, I'll explain it to them, and maybe I'll show them the photos and other bits I collected in memory of our darling twins.

TONI'S STORY

WITH MY second pregnancy, I had a miscarriage at eight weeks. I had been spotting for a week or so beforehand, but I went for an ultrasound and I could see the heartbeat; everything looked good. No matter what anyone else believed regarding the stage at which an embryo becomes a baby, this was my unborn child. One week later my baby died, and I cried for days.

In my next pregnancy, the nightmare began again at about seven weeks, when I started spotting. I was so worried that I was going to lose this baby as well, but an ultrasound revealed a good possibility that the "problem" was being absorbed. Soon afterwards the spotting ceased, and the pregnancy seemed to be going well, until I went for my eighteen-week ultrasound. As the nurse looked at the monitor, she told us that we had a healthy baby but that there was also something else there that didn't look right.

Two scans later they discovered that I was carrying identical twins, but one of them had not developed as expected; he had no heart and his brain had not developed, but he was alive and moving. Apparently the healthy twin was providing him with blood via the placenta—the chances of this happening are only one in every eighty thousand pregnancies. Sadly, this was not the worst news for us. We were told that because of the extra workload placed on the healthy twin, there was a 50 percent chance of heart failure for him. We knew then that we might lose both of our little ones. Each week I had to go for an ultrasound in order to monitor and detect early signs of heart failure. Although we knew that there were methods of intervention available if heart failure was detected, they were methods that had been tried only a few times around the world, and they were still experimental. We lived week by week, hoping I would reach the benchmark whereby my healthy baby would live even if he had to be delivered early.

Eventually, we found that the weaker twin had started to collect fluid and swell. His weight increased to over three kilograms, and as a result the healthier twin had less space and was being squashed. There was no choice left but to deliver the boys by cesarean section at twenty-nine weeks. Alexander Paul did not make it, but Darcy, his darling brother, is now a year old. He spent the first ten weeks of his life in special care and intensive care units and has since had two operations. Today, although he is small for his age, has a moderate hearing loss, and is unable, as yet, to sit unsupported, he is our little miracle boy. All that matters is that he is with us now.

Since then our priorities in life have changed significantly, and we have realized how much is taken for granted when it comes to having healthy children. When others say they don't care whether their baby is a boy or a girl, as long as he or she is healthy, it really hits home for us. We don't just pay lip service to that statement; it means something.

CHERYL'S STORY

EVERYTHING ABOUT my pregnancy was normal until I went into labor. When I arrived at the hospital, they discovered that the baby was breech and realized that this could cause difficulties in the delivery. The staff called my husband, but the baby wasn't prepared to wait for his arrival, and they took me into the operating theater for an emergency cesarean. Before they gave me the general anesthetic, the nurse asked me if there was anything I wanted to tell my baby, and my immediate response was, Tell him to be healthy.

By the time Mike arrived at the hospital, our little boy had been born and Mike was told that our baby wasn't going to live;

the term they used for his condition was "incompatible with life." The nurse then asked Mike if he would like to name our baby and have him baptized. As I was just waking up from the surgery, he decided to wait before making any decisions about the name, but he baptized the baby and said to him, "We don't have a name for you yet, but God will recognize you when you get there."

When I woke up, they told me what was happening, and before my son died I was able to hold him and tell him how much I loved him. We named him John, and the worst thing for me was knowing that I was his mom but not being able to do anything to help him. Now, instead of making plans for our new life together as a family, we were being asked about burial arrangements, miniature cemetery plots, and miniature caskets. The final decision was which clothes we would bury our precious little son in. I had neatly folded and arranged all of his little socks and outfits; everything was waiting for him to come home, but now he wasn't here. The only things I had were secondhand clothes that my mother had found for him at various garage sales. She had loved garage sales, but I still felt awful that I didn't have anything new to dress him in.

Then, as I thought about it more, I realized that dressing him in one of the outfits she had chosen for him was the nicest thing I could do. My mother had died two months earlier from breast cancer. She had so wanted to live to see our baby, but as hard as the doctors tried, they had been unable to keep her alive. I get some comfort from knowing that his grandma was waiting for him in Heaven.

Losing a baby has changed me, I think more than I realize. After you've held your baby in your arms as he draws his last breath, it's hard to get upset about fingerprints on the windows or crumbs in the car.

VANESSA'S STORY

NINE YEARS ago, I got pregnant for the first time, and when I went for an ultrasound, I was told there were two. "Two what?" I said. "Two babies," was the reply. I can't explain in words how overjoyed and shocked Andrew and I were; we just felt incredibly special and fortunate to be having twins.

Our joy was short-lived, though, when at only twenty-eight weeks I went into labor. After a very anxious three-hour trip in an ambulance on a wet and stormy night, we arrived at the hospital just as the babies decided it was time to arrive. The birth was so quick I lay there in shock, thinking, Why is this happening to us? We were told our boys didn't have a very good chance of survival, as their lungs were not developed enough to be able to breathe on their own. They were both placed on ventilators, but, sadly, Aaron, our firstborn little boy, died seven days after entering the world, and Wade, his brother, died fifty-two days later.

Andrew and I stayed in the neonatal unit with them for the entire time, and what we saw and experienced in all those harrowing days will never be lost in my memory. Not only were our children struggling to survive, but so many other tiny babies with their devoted parents were going through such an emotional roller coaster. My husband was strongly affected by what was happening to his little boys, and I tried to support him as much as possible, but it was so difficult, because I actually felt responsible for his grief. It was very hard to cope with all this sadness, but we had to be strong for each other.

It became increasingly difficult to hang on to hope and to be positive for so many days when we knew there was such a slim chance of the boys' survival. We were fortunate, at least, to be able to nurse and cuddle our tiny babies as they died. It was not an easy time, but we were able to say our goodbyes and to really hold them close for the first, and last, time—a time we will never forget.

What did I do wrong? Was it my fault that our little children had died? My specialist told us there was no known reason why they came early, so now, when I look back, I become angry and frustrated with the way it was all handled. As it was my first pregnancy, I really didn't know what to expect and how I should feel; my doctor said nothing about the risk of carrying multiples close to full term and how important it is to take it easy through the last half of the pregnancy.

Three months after the loss of our boys, I became pregnant again, and we had a beautiful baby girl—Emily, who is now nine years old. Two years after her birth, I became pregnant with twins again, and throughout the pregnancy we remained anxious and concerned for fear that tragedy might strike again. I stayed in bed for the last three months, and to our joy, our twins Samuel and Brianna were born healthy and perfect.

CATHY'S STORY

I WILL never forget my first pregnancy, which ended abruptly at ten weeks. I can't help but wonder what might have been for that child, what he or she might have looked like, and I still shed a silent tear whenever I think about what happened.

After six months of marriage, we were surprised and thrilled to find out we were pregnant. Although we had intended to wait about two years before starting a family, we were very excited at the thought of becoming parents. I come from a large family, and no woman in my family has had trouble conceiving, seemingly sailing through pregnancy and producing healthy children. Therefore, it simply didn't occur to me to hold off spreading the good news for the first twelve weeks in case something happened. Of course I knew about miscarriage, and I even knew some women who had experienced it, but I just assumed it would never happen to me. I also assumed—wrongly, with hindsight—that it was something women "got over."

Everything was fine until I reached ten weeks, and then, one afternoon, I noticed I'd started spotting. I was advised by my doctor to take bed rest, which I did, but the bleeding became heavier, and finally my husband took me to the emergency unit at our local hospital. After four long hours, a doctor finally saw me. I had an internal examination and was told that my cervix was still closed, so I should go home and back to bed.

The bleeding continued, and my husband and I became increasingly worried, until one night I found I couldn't sleep and got up. I had bad back pain and cramping, so I made up a hotwater bottle and prepared to watch a bit of television. Then, when I stood up to go to the toilet, I realized that blood was running down my leg, and I only just made it to the bathroom as the contents of my uterus fell into the toilet. My husband woke up to my screams and immediately took me to the hospital, where they cleaned me up and admitted me to a ward.

Later that day I met the doctor who was going to perform the dilation and curettage, and then I was wheeled into the operating theater. When I woke up two hours later, I just felt empty inside, and when I left to go home, I felt as though I'd left something behind. I guess I was unprepared for all the raw emotions that came over me, and I cried for what seemed like an eternity. My husband was equally devastated, but although he wanted to cry, he seemed unable to. The whole thing was so traumatic, neither of us could face getting pregnant again quickly.

When we got home, we were inundated with well-meaning relatives helping out with the house and offering words of wisdom. Everyone seemed to have some kind of theory or tired old cliche to explain away the loss, but they all seemed so wrong to me. In hindsight, Lucas and I should have spent that time alone, time together when we could have talked and cried and held each other.

LEE-ANN'S STORY

UPSTAIRS IN my filing cabinet under the letter B are the memories of my third baby. Often I will pull out the yellow business-size envelope that holds those precious memories of the baby I never held in my arms. I have my ankle tag, a foot- and a handprint of my baby, two cards from friends, my pathology card, and a letter from a supportive mother to remind me that it was not all a dream. Our whole family was thrilled at the news that I was pregnant again, and almost immediately we started to make plans for the birth. At the time I was doing two jobs, and the work was stressful, but as my two previous pregnancies had been relatively easy, I thought nothing of it and managed my workload around everything else that was happening in my life.

Even though I was thirty-six years old, I decided against intrusive tests like amniocentesis and instead elected to have an ultrasound. I lay on the bed anxiously awaiting the ultrasonographer, who when he arrived was very pleasant and explained the whole procedure to us, including the fact that it should take about thirty minutes. I was surprised, then, when after only five minutes he helped me up and told me to get dressed. I didn't know what was happening, but when my husband told me that the doctor had said it wasn't good news, I knew the nightmare had begun.

Waiting in a small room for the doctor to join us seemed like an eternity. The glossy magazines lying on the table held no interest for me, as my senses were heightened; I heard my own heartbeat and felt the eyes of the nurses opposite looking at me. My world was crashing in on me as we waited dumbfounded for the doctor. The doctor came in at last and broke the terrible news to us. The baby had no heartbeat; it had been dead for at least two weeks.

I hope I never have to go back to that place again. My heart was torn out, my world had crumbled around me, and I was walking but not seeing. I was alone and yet with my husband and I was carrying a dead baby inside me. I remember rushing out of the hospital and standing near the car feeling trapped, wanting to run but being unable to do so. All the way home I rubbed my bump and kept saying, "My baby is dead."

We went to a city hospital three days later. It was necessary to have a specialist remove the baby under a general anesthetic, using ultrasound, as my previous babies had been delivered by cesarean. For this operation I was induced beforehand, and I decided to have morphine. At least then the emotional as well as the physical pain would be numbed. I shall always be grateful to the hospital social worker who talked to me about my loss and suggested that I get my daughter's hand- and footprints. Because of her I have what are now my only tangible links to my tiny daughter.

I often used to wonder why other women who have had children do not understand what it feels like to have a miscarriage. Surely they would know, I used to think, but now I know they don't know. It is like being accepted into a very exclusive club, and the only way to enter is by direct experience. In all of this it is the women who have lost babies who have touched my heart and supported me—with a knowing look, a touch of the hand, or a reminder of their own loss, however long ago it was.

I have decided to have those tiny little hand- and footprints framed and to hang them on a wall in our house so that the family can be reminded of our little one. I will never forget; others already have.

Equally important, for those of us fortunate enough to go on and have a child, is coming to terms with the fact that no new baby can take the place of the child or children we have lost. All that might have been for one child cannot be transposed onto our subsequent children, whether we are talking about their character, features, or potential achievements. Knowing this, however, does not always guarantee our ability to accept the child we do have as a completely separate individual, to love that child unconditionally and without any sense of guilt at his or her existence. This can be particularly difficult when the time frame is such that, had the one baby lived, the new baby could not have been conceived. We need to be able to accept the baby we hold in our arms as a precious gift wrapped in love, leaving no room for any guilt at all.

In this respect I suppose I was lucky. My eldest daughter, Elizabeth, could not have been born had the twins made it to term; she was conceived the month before their due date, because I couldn't wait a moment longer. But she was one child, not two. The twins had been a unit, an entity in themselves, and so Elizabeth was very different. The problem is more likely to arise when the surviving baby is the same sex, almost a mirror image of the baby who died.

DEBORAH'S STORY

I BECAME pregnant in 1995 with our first child—an accident, but very much wanted nonetheless. My husband, Patrick, and I had been married for five years, and we were what others referred to as older parents—he was thirty-nine and I was thirty-four. Everything with the pregnancy seemed to progress well except for my morning sickness, which lasted for eighteen weeks. My first ultrasound was fine, and I was seeing my doctor regularly, but something at the back of my mind was nagging away at me. I worried that something was wrong, because I had not felt a lot of movement.

I continued to work through the pregnancy, and my husband and I commuted daily into the city. At a little over twenty-four weeks, I started to bleed while I was at work and I rushed to the local hospital, where I was taken into the labor ward. A midwife examined me, but as she had difficulty finding a heartbeat, she went off to find a doctor. When the doctor arrived, she was very kind. She too looked for the heartbeat and then placed her hand on mine and explained that I would have to go for an ultrasound, but to expect the worst. I lay there thinking, The worst what? It just didn't dawn on me that the baby could be dead.

By this time Patrick had arrived at the hospital, and I went to the waiting room where he was and told him what was happening. I can still remember the look of utter shock on his face as he threw himself back into the chair and cried. We went together for the ultrasound, and I watched as the woman performing it started to point out our baby's arms and legs. But he was lying so still and looked so lonely I said to her, "Is my baby dead?" She said, "Yes, your baby is dead." My world crashed, and as I started to cry, Patrick covered my eyes with his hands.

We were then taken into another room, where the doctor explained that they would have to induce labor—it would be long and painful, but I would be able to have as much pain relief as I needed. I remember everything that was said to me at that moment, but I felt as though I no longer inhabited my own body; it was someone else who was listening and someone else who was asking all the questions. Anyway, we decided to be admitted immediately and begin the induction, and nineteen hours later our child was born.

As I leaned down to grab the baby, Patrick pushed me back and covered my eyes; he had decided that I shouldn't see our little one, and as I was so frightened, I allowed him to take control of every-thing. To this day I regret what happened, especially as I was later offered the opportunity by a counselor to hold the baby and to arrange a funeral for him and I turned both opportunities down.

We came home, and that was when it finally hit me. That gap-ing wound deep within my soul was like no other pain I had ever experienced in my life, and I spent the day wandering around the house screaming for my son. I felt I would never get over what had happened. Patrick fielded the many calls and took the flow-ers and cards as they started to arrive. He fed me and let me scream and then he held me.

In 1997 I became pregnant again, but at eight weeks I miscar-ried. The pain in my heart returned, and I felt as though I had nothing in my life; I felt such a dismal failure. I even told my hus-band that if he wanted to leave me I would understand, but his answer was that he had me and that was the most important thing to him. He had tremendous hope and believed in his heart that we would become parents.

Then, two months later, we were pregnant again. With all the old fears and worries coming rushing back, I remained reluctant to acknowledge the pregnancy until, at about twenty weeks, I started to get those wonderful fluttery feelings and I knew my child was alive. I rested, I read, and I ate well, and finally, in 1998, our beautiful son Alexander was born. Unfortunately, they had to perform a cesarean section, as my blood pressure became alarmingly high towards the end of my labor. I had expected to be able to give birth naturally, so I crumpled. It was very painful, and I found when our baby was born that I had no feelings for him or any notion of bonding with him.

I remember the first night, after Patrick had left the hospital, when I lay there with our new son beside me in his crib. We were looking directly at each other, and I started to cry, because, after all I had been through, it was not him I wanted; I wanted my first son, and I felt so guilty. Three days after his birth, I went to pieces, and the nursing staff became concerned about postnatal depression, so they moved me to a private room. I was having great difficulty breast-feeding, and I was so tired and exhausted and in such pain from the operation.

When I left the hospital, I slowly regained my strength with the help of family and friends, but it took eight weeks before I finally looked at Alexander and felt a huge rush of fierce, protec-tive, overwhelming love and happiness at having him as a part of our lives. I sat and held him so close and rocked him as my tears spilled onto his little baby cheeks. I had been so convinced that I would never have those feelings for him.

I also started to attend SANDS (Stillbirth and Neonatal Death Support) meetings soon after I arrived home, and I still go to them, as they have been a tremendous help. It is only there I feel I can talk openly about my children and not be judged. I feel I have come a long way, although I still feel incredible hurt when I think about what happened. Some days I feel God has chosen me to go through this for a reason, and I think it was to make me stop and think and to be more compassionate and listen, really listen, to others' problems and feelings.

I will carry with me until my dying day the regret and remorse that I never held and said goodbye to Syd and that we didn't give him a funeral. I can't go back, though, so I'm learning to live with those regrets. I know now that I should have held him and I should have laid him to rest properly, but I find it a tremendous comfort to know that my son is waiting for me. When I take my last breath, he will be standing there waiting to take my hand, and his soul will be with me again. Then, at last, I will know him.

JACINTA'S STORY

AFTER OUR first pregnancy ended in a miscarriage at eight weeks, my husband, Matt, and I were delighted when two months later I got pregnant again. Although I had morning sickness throughout the pregnancy, it didn't worry me, as I saw it as a good sign. My mother and sisters had suffered in a similar way, so I really didn't think it was unusual.

At about thirty weeks, my hands and feet became very swollen, but my obstetrician assured me that this was a normal part of pregnancy. When the swelling continued and it became clear that the aches, pains, morning sickness, and insomnia were getting me down, he arranged for me to be induced two days before my due date. I was so thankful that the end was near.

On the morning I was due to go into the hospital, I went into labor naturally, and Matt rushed me to the labor ward. My baby was on its way, but from the moment it became obvious that neither the midwife nor my obstetrician could find a heartbeat, everything started to go wrong. The next few hours were a blur as they took gallons of blood for testing and gave me pethidine for the pain. The night went on and on, until finally Patrick was born. I remember the silence—there was no crying, his or mine.

Matt's parents and brother and my parents had arrived to be

with us, and we each held Patrick. Mum also called our local priest, who came and blessed Patrick, naming him for us. I will always be grateful to the extraordinary group of women who looked after us. Patrick didn't miss out on anything any living baby would have had. He had his name bands on his wrists, a name card on his hospital bed, and he was able to wear his own clothes. I didn't miss out either; I bathed him, changed his diaper, and dressed him just as any other mother would have done.

Finally, the next evening, the time came for us to say goodbye. It was the hardest thing I've ever had to do, knowing that I would never see my baby boy again. I was discharged from the hospital four days later, the funeral arrangements were made, and Patrick was brought home to the country to be buried.

Although it was hard, we tried to get on with our lives, and three months later I became pregnant again. This time it was a little girl. I tried to tell people that I couldn't replace Patrick when this baby was a girl. I don't know if they believed me or not. In August 1998, Phoebe was born—a perfectly healthy, happy, and very much alive little baby, but the first six weeks with her were so hard. I was still in the hospital for the first anniversary of Patrick's death, and my feelings were so confused. I now had a beautiful baby girl who had arrived in this world safely; I had everything I asked for, yet I still wasn't happy. Today, I still feel sad, because I love this little person so much, but I should have another child running around and throwing toddler tantrums.

Phoebe is now seven months old, and she is the most gorgeous person you've ever met. She has such a happy, smiley personality, and I love every minute I spend with her. The pain never goes away, but I believe that these things happen for a reason. The answer will probably not show itself to me in this lifetime, but eventually all things will be revealed, and I will understand. In the meantime, Matt and I believe that Patrick went through all the babies and sent us the best one.

LYNN'S STORY

I EXPERIENCED a miscarriage in 1995, after three uneventful, healthy pregnancies that produced my three sons. I gave birth to my twins when I was only sixteen weeks pregnant, after battling a group B streptococcus infection; the labor was long and difficult, and I nearly lost my own life. Apparently I was allergic to the morphine they gave me for the pain, and therefore I experienced respiratory distress during labor and a cardiac arrest during the dilation and curettage later.

I mourned the loss of my babies and especially the loss of my daughter, as for more than ten years I had dreamed of having a daughter. Eventually, though, I realized that they had been taken from me and that I had survived for a reason. I just needed to wait and see what that reason was. Two years later, I delivered my fourth son at only twenty-seven weeks' gestation. He weighed two pounds, nine ounces, and for the next two and a half months he battled for his life as he lay in the neonatal intensive care unit. Today he is a happy three-year-old with cerebral palsy—the result of oxygen loss experienced during his traumatic birth.

I now know the reason for the past pain of my miscarriage; it was so that I could be the fighter my son needs me to be. I never cry over the "normal" child I felt I "deserved"; I rejoice over the beautiful little boy I was given. He has made me the mother I have always wanted to be—patient, tolerant, and loving—but most of all, he makes me move a little slower. He lets me see all the wonders I used to rush by and miss. Quite simply, he makes me, and he makes our family, whole.

When you reach for the moon, you'll at least get stars!

SUSAN'S STORY

WHEN MY husband and I were posted to Seoul, we already had a fifteen-month-old son when we discovered I was pregnant again. All seemed to go well until the ninth week, when I started to bleed, and although I rested in bed, I could not save my baby. Late one night I started to get terrible cramping, and as I sat on the toilet, I caught what was my nine-week-old baby on a wad of toilet paper. I then did something I shall always regret; I put it in the toilet and flushed it away. As soon as I'd done it, I knew I shouldn't have, and even today I am tormented with feelings of guilt and shame.

Feeling empty and full of grief, I returned home, and life continued, as it must, while I pretended to be happy with my little boy, all the while trying to stop the ache in my heart. Just three months later I got pregnant again, and it was a completely different pregnancy, with constant nausea, swollen breasts, etc. Forty-one and a half weeks later, Emily Elizabeth arrived, rather reluctantly, it seemed. She's an absolute joy and spends her whole time seeking attention with smiles and chats; if that fails, we get the indignant screams. Nothing delights her more than to be held, smiled at, and caressed. She is my last baby, and I try to hold on to the moments I have with her, yet she's already six months old. It's the quiet, private times I have with her that sometimes become overwhelming, because I know if I hadn't lost my second baby, Emily would not exist. I find this shocking and frightening, as I cannot imagine life without her. The feeling makes me feel guilty about her very existence—the fact that she was born only because of a loss—and I wonder if she senses it and therefore tries even harder to make her presence felt. Then sometimes I wonder whether I deliberately keep her close to fill the void.

I would dearly love to know if I had been going to be the mother of another girl or another boy. I wonder what his or her character and soul would have been like, but there are no answers, so, it seems, no closure. Having Emily didn't heal the pain—in some ways it complicated things. She is precious for her uniqueness, and my family is now complete, but my lost baby will be remembered forever and wondered about and missed, so completely missed.

VICKI'S STORY

DO YOU know or can you not see the pain that you cause when you dismiss my loss as trivial? Do you not realize that although they are merely words, it still cuts like a knife when you tell me everything is fine because it wasn't really a baby I lost? As far as

I'm concerned, it was a baby, and I am that child's mother. Just because you do not acknowledge it does not make it any less real to me.

Just what is it that makes a baby real, and who of us gets to decide? According to the dictionary, *real* is defined as "existing in fact, not imagined or supposed." However, there may also be another meaning, as explained in the children's story, *The Velveteen Rabbit*.

You see, the velveteen rabbit was a toy rabbit that belonged to a small boy. The toy dreamed of becoming a real rabbit, but, being a toy, he didn't know how to become real—or indeed if he was real already. He pondered these questions until his friend the skin horse gave him the answer. It went something like this: "Real is not how you are made, but something you become once you are truly loved by someone. That love makes you real."

Of course, once a toy is truly loved, it often looks quite shabby and may appear to us to be less than perfect, yet, to the one who loves it, it is beautiful. Whether it has lost its eyes or its nose or whether it is falling apart matters not to the person who loves it.

Once again the skin horse spoke to the velveteen rabbit: "That doesn't matter, because you are real and you cannot be ugly, except to those who don't understand."

So you see, the little velveteen rabbit wasn't a toy. He was real to the little boy, and that is all that really mattered. Likewise, while my baby is not all that you perceive a baby to be, to me that child could be no more real even if it were here with me now.

My love makes my baby real to me, so shouldn't that make it real to you also?

Rachael with Daisies

I've brought you Easter daisies.
In the autumn garden, looking at the tattered fringe
of lilies and the droop of brown-edged roses,
I was surprised by starwhite: the daisies
had arranged by night their private spring.
They do it every year, of course, about this time,
but somehow I'd forgotten.

They seemed appropriate, but now I'm here
I do not think that I can bear to lay
their fragile promise on your two small graves.

(BY BARBARA, IN MEMORY OF HER TWINS)

A Shared Loss

*A*FTER SIMON AND CLARE DIED, I WAS COMFORTED as the flowers and letters began to flood into our home. It wasn't important, at that point, that most of my family and friends didn't really understand how I was feeling. It was enough that they had taken the time to show they cared, and it provided me with a kind of invisible blanket of protection against some of the pain I was going to have to face after the initial shock dissipated.

But while I was wrapped in the knowledge that others were there for me, I didn't realize that Peter wasn't enjoying a similar sense of empathy from them. I was shocked, therefore, when he pointed out that all the cards that came with the flowers and all the letters that people had taken the time to write were addressed to me alone. All he said was, "They were my babies too." And while he didn't make a big issue out of his feelings of disappointment at the time, all these years later it is something he remembers and is still saddened by.

High on the list of expectations we have for the modern man is that he adopt a more involved role in the home and family. This expectation is by no means unreasonable, but, in return, we must acknowledge his part in the parenting process, and therefore his grief when impending fatherhood is snatched from him. All too often, others—and this can include his partner—fail to see just how much he is hurting. This is not due to a lack of care; it is often due to a failure to understand exactly how great an emotional impact losing a child has on him. We can't deny that the majority of adult men have been brought up to behave in ways that are strong, tough, unbreakable, incapable of deep sorrow, and free from emotional baggage. These are now outdated expectations of manhood that make the open expression of grief unacceptable.

It is hard enough for most men to externalize their emotions through tears or words, but doing so is made even more difficult if a man sees the attention, the flowers, and the care generally being directed toward the mother. When this happens, those traditional expectations he was brought up with are reaffirmed, and instead of reaching out for love and support in his own right, he gives what he has left to his partner. The tragedy is that he is often left wanting.

From the hundreds of letters I received when researching this book, only a handful came from men, and yet hearing their side of the story is paramount to our understanding of this subject. I applaud those men who have opened their hearts to us simply for having the strength not to succumb to others' expectations. These are extraordinary men, in whose experiences I am proud to have been allowed to share.

RICHARD'S STORY

WHEN YOUR child dies, it is natural to want to blame someone. The harsh truth, however, is that a significant number of premature babies do die despite the best efforts of the medical staff. I know, because it happened to us.

Our son Oliver died in November 1998, after entering this world three and a half months too early. My wife, Jacqui, had developed an infection in her womb, and when that happens, the body's natural defense system urges the expulsion of the unborn child.

It was every expectant parent's worst nightmare. I was in the office when the panicked phone call came through: Jacqui's waters had broken outside the Great Portland Street tube station in London. The due date was not until late February. Luckily, Jacqui was with a friend, who took her to University College Hospital, in central London. The doctors confirmed that her waters had broken, but said that labor had not yet begun. If she could just hold off for even twelve hours, it would give the baby a greater chance of survival.

Jacqui struggled valiantly for almost forty-eight hours, allowing the doctors to give her two doses of steroids to aid the development of the child's lungs. The odds were not good; twenty-four weeks was the "cusp of viability," said the consultant. At this point of development, only four in ten babies survive the delivery.

By late afternoon of the second day, Jacqui had entered labor. Unfortunately, her temperature rocketed and she contracted a raging fever. We had to open the windows and brandish electric fans to bring her temperature down to a reasonable level. I stood in the corridor as the midwife told me the complications meant that the baby would not live. Nevertheless, my wife had to go through the labor, and at 9:26 P.M. on November 1st—rather spookily my own birthday and within thirty minutes of the time of my delivery—Oliver was born. Although he was gray, limp, and voiceless and weighed less than a bag of sugar, the pediatrician succeeded in reviving our son, and he was transferred to intensive care.

There, under ultraviolet lights and accompanied by the airline ping of the computers, I had the first real opportunity to see my son. At twenty-four weeks, a baby's skin is not fully formed, so the nurses had stretched a plastic tent over Oliver to retain the moisture. But beneath the plastic was a perfectly formed, divine-looking little boy.

Then began the roller-coaster ride of our lives: would Oliver's heart and lungs be strong enough to keep him alive? We forced ourselves to view each successive hour as a bonus—after all, no one had expected him to make it through the delivery—while deep down we were willing him, praying for him to survive this ordeal so that he might stay with us.

A great many children born so prematurely die within forty-eight hours of delivery. Some do not survive the move downstairs to the neonatal unit. Their hearts fail or, more commonly, their lungs stop functioning, even with the best ventilator. Oliver survived this initial period—both his heart and lungs were strong—but tests revealed that he had suffered acute brain damage, either during his time in the womb or during delivery. As the days passed, the nature of this damage became apparent, and our joy at his survival evaporated.

Even a baby who stays in the womb for the whole nine months does not have a fully developed brain; it takes another twelve months to assume its final form. In Oliver's case, the parts of the brain that control movement were so badly damaged that they would never recover. If he survived, he would never be able to walk, he would never do anything that normal children do, not even hold a knife and fork. He might never speak.

At the same time, the doctors discovered that his bowels were perforated and that he had contracted necrotizing enterocolitis (NEC), a potentially fatal condition and a common killer of premature babies. In these circumstances, the doctors asked us to think carefully about whether it was right to keep Oliver alive by artificial means. In their opinion, the kindest act would be to let him go.

After much soul searching, we decided that the doctors were right. My greatest fear was that Oliver would have a healthy mind trapped in a useless body. In any event, as the postmortem examination would later show, our boy would almost certainly have died from his bowel condition. We had him christened in the ward, and then, on the following Sunday, almost seven days after he came into this world, the medical staff unplugged Oliver from the life-support machinery. We held him—our first real opportunity to do so without the encumbrance of the ventilator—while he died.

Neither Jacqui nor I recall being asked to sign a consent form for any of Oliver's treatments, although a researcher gently asked if she might monitor his brain patterns for a study. We agreed. Frankly, we would have leapt at any treatment suggested by the doctors if they'd thought it would improve Oliver's chances of survival. As for the medical staff, both doctors and nurses were superb, doing their utmost for Oliver while offering us tremendous emotional support. They were visibly upset by his death; one or two were in tears as we said our last goodbyes.

No one really knew what to say to us. Many people lacked the requisite language. While politics, religion, and sex are now acceptable topics of conversation, infant mortality is still strictly off-limits, the last conversational taboo.

Some people said, "Never mind, you'll have other children." The point was that we wanted this child. Others decided to deal with us as if nothing had happened. There were exceptions. Our best friends, Clare and Ant, were pillars of strength throughout the ordeal, often bedding down in the hospital with us. At work, our colleagues were also very supportive and understanding, particularly Jacqui's associates. Many were so moved that they made charitable donations to the neonatal unit. The best simply said, "We are thinking of you."

We were both surprised, however, to learn just how many other people had experienced a similar tragedy. We have found ourselves members of a club for which no one willingly signs up. If things had gone according to plan, Oliver would have been with us now. Instead, he lies under a yew tree in the cemetery, surrounded by other unfortunate children. We feel guilty because we do not visit him regularly. We know of other parents who go once a week. But the truth is that we do not know what to say when we stand beside his tiny grave, and it is just too painful. Instead, the handful of pictures we have of Oliver are proudly displayed around our apartment. Some people might think we are strange, even morbid, to display them, but he was and always will be our first child and our first son.

As the ancient Romans believed, if my name is on someone's lips, I am still alive.

David's Story

It was the slam of the screen door that jolted me awake. My wife staggered inside and whispered, "You'll have to get me to the hospital, now!" I threw on my clothes and woke up my infant son. As I carried him over to my father's cabin, the tears started to flow. I knew in my heart that our world was falling apart.

My wife, Tiffany, had been bleeding intermittently for around a week. Some five weeks earlier, she had had some cramping and slightly heavier bleeding, but that had all gone away. The morning sickness had seemingly finished, and everything was looking good. Even the latest bleeding was not uncommon in early pregnancy, according to our local general practitioner. Well, here we were, at five o'clock in the morning, driving to the hospital with the dreadful knowledge that something was very wrong.

At the hospital, Tiffany was ushered immediately to a bed. Thus began the procession of doctors and nurses poking and prodding, a process that would continue well into the evening. The night staff did what they could while the regional doctor was called. After what seemed like an eternity, he arrived and commenced his own examination. When he requested an ultrasound, I didn't want to ask him about the prognosis. Even to my untrained eye, it was apparent that no one could bleed so heavily without disastrous consequences.

The X-ray department was quiet at this early hour, so we were swiftly ushered in for an ultrasound. The moment of truth had arrived. Although I had known the probable outcome, my heart still yearned for a positive result. But the monitor confirmed my worst fears: there was our baby, halfway down the now open birth canal. The doctor saw a "nonviable pregnancy"; I saw the death of our hopes and dreams. The pain inside me was crushing. Here was our precious child, the fullness of our love for each other, lifeless.

There was nothing I could do to protect my baby, no way I could shield my child in my strong arms and breathe life back into his lungs. I did not even know if my baby was a boy or a girl. The grief finally overwhelmed me, and I collapsed sobbing into my wife's embrace.

Tiffany then had to have an operation to remove the last traces of precious life. The day had already seemed to last a lifetime, and now this! As I waited for the surgery to end, the questions raged once again. Why did this happen to us? Why does it hurt so much? Will this emptiness ever go away?

I could not understand the intensity of the pain I was feeling. We had known about the pregnancy for only a few short weeks. We had never seen this baby, had not felt a movement, had never held him in our arms, never heard his cry, yet the ache of loss engulfed my very being. I wanted to crawl into my bed and escape, but I knew that I had to be there when my wife awoke. As bad as I was feeling, she would be suffering even greater loss. I put my hurts aside and set about comforting my wife, still groggy from the anesthetic.

The remainder of that period passed in a haze. There was no real time to grieve. This would come in stages, but one good thing was that, having taken some time off work, we were able to spend time working through a whole range of emotions. The most astounding thing to emerge from this tragedy was that, in a matter of days, more than thirty women we knew told us they too had suffered up to eight miscarriages each. Of all these women, we had known only about one prior to our own experience.

All of a sudden I started to comprehend the extent of this occurrence. While I was thinking that no one could possibly understand what we were going through, more than half the couples we knew had been through exactly the same thing. Why had they not spoken about it? Talking to us and just sharing emotions and experiences was so liberating, not only for us, but also for the women who had not addressed their own past hurts. They were able to grieve with us and heal with us as well.

Within a few short weeks, both my cousin and a friend went through a similar tragedy. On each occasion, Tiffany and I worked through a little more of our own hurt by simply being there for them. No words were necessary; just being there for each other was enough.

As time elapsed, I began to question the whole issue of miscarriage and why it remained such an apparently forbidden subject. I could not understand why people did not share their experiences with each other. The numbers of people affected are staggering, yet those people who have been lucky enough not to experience miscarriage remain blissfully unaware of its prevalence. According to the medical profession, well in excess of half of all miscarriages are the result of a physical or mental abnormality in the unborn child. Although this helps to understand the reasons, this alone does not make the parents involved feel any better. Their dreams have been shattered. They have lived to see the death of their child. Never make the cruel mistake of assuming that, just because the baby was not yet born, the pain is any less than with any other loss.

Before our own experience, a close friend's wife had a miscarriage very soon after finding out that she was pregnant. I had no concept of what they were going through, and I can still hear my pathetic condolences as I tried to reassure him that it was better for it to happen so early rather than later in the pregnancy or, worse, after the birth. The tragedy is that so many of us do the same. We cannot understand why parents grieve so deeply for someone they never knew. I can't explain it, but suffice to say we do. We need the support of family and friends; we do not need platitudes, we just need to talk, and we need someone to listen.

If anyone you know goes through such an experience, please remember the agony and the grief they are certainly experiencing. Allow them to cry, allow them to talk, and don't assume that they want answers from you. None of us can give the answers, but we can enable the parents to move on by giving selfless love and support.

Tiffany and I now have another baby in our arms, and we consider ourselves privileged to have been able to help other people through such terrible times in their lives. The pain will never go, but the passage of time brings with it a new outlook. I know that my precious babe is right now being comforted in the arms of the Lord himself and that one day I will meet my child face to face.

DENIS'S STORY

MY WIFE bore premature children. It's not the worst thing that can happen to parents or would-be parents, but it's enough.

Suzanne and I have had two preemies and one "nearly." Samantha, the first, was the nearly. She beat the defined barriers by a week and nine ounces, so she was fairly early, but not a problem. Adam came nearly two years later, in Papua, New Guinea, and he was in too much of a hurry by a long shot. More than ten weeks early, he was reckoned to have about one chance in three of surviving. He came in the early hours of the morning after a quick labor for Suzanne. It's hard to believe, when you see such an apparently perfectly formed little being born to a frightened, unprepared mother, that he won't live very long. Not much earlier and he would have been the anonymous result of a miscarriage. Although at the time I thought that would have been easier, I know now that it's not. Losing a child at any stage of pregnancy is equally sad for the parents.

As a premature baby, however, he was far enough along the human trail to yell when he was rather hurriedly born. Weighing something under two pounds, he didn't take much bearing. A skinny, wrinkled, mottled red and purple thing, he still had features you could see as your own—hands and feet, the family nose, an earlobe. He was immediately mine.

I saw the doctor's face, after concentrating for some indeterminate time on my wife's to encourage her, and I hadn't seen him so serious looking before. He poked a plastic tube in the baby's face, worried, to do the usual clearing of passages. I thought it was because the baby wasn't breathing, but he was. Minutes passed, with stethoscope and fingers probing, feeling.

"He seems all right," the doctor said eventually, guardedly, and the operating theater nurse put him into an incubator. "He cried straight off, and that's a good sign. We won't really know how he'll go for twenty-four hours, perhaps forty-eight. That's the critical time. He seems all there, but he's on the edge of survival. He looks good, but on statistics I have to tell you he can't be given an even chance. You must not be too optimistic yet." The doctor grimaced, partly out of sympathy for us and partly out of sheer helplessness. All this I was told while standing outside the operating theater door, and I had to find the words to explain it all to Suzanne as she held tightly on to my hand.

There was nothing for her to do but worry, so despite her unwillingness, they tranquilized her. She wanted to stay awake and fight the battle with him, but the doctors knew that she'd need all her strength later; not experiencing the depths of feelings at that point would help her afterwards. Nobody knew how long a battle there'd be, so she'd better get some rest. Before I went to get a few hours' sleep myself, we decided that the time was right to name our son, regardless of the outcome. Adam was to be our first son and this was he. It wouldn't seem right to keep the name for another.

I left the hospital and saw the soft gray traces of dawn. Dawn, new life, and all that. Too many Victorian novels? I was exhilarated at having seen my son born in front of me, at having at last helped Suzanne about as much as a husband can at birth, at being needed for moral support more than I anticipated. I was frightened, too, and shook with fear and weariness. Before sleeping, I prayed briefly and fiercely, then used once more my greatest blessing—quick sleep.

People told of the night's events, almost to a man. had a sudden shadow over their faces. You can tell people about almost any other trouble or sadness and you'll get a mixed reaction. But the thought of a tiny human being hanging on precariously to life brings very different reactions: "What do I say? What can I do?" their faces and voices tell you.

During the day, the sun blazing and the temperature reaching for its usual ninety degrees, I decided to photograph Adam as he lay in his incubator. Whatever happened, I wanted to remember this day.

Again I visited the hospital and looked long and hard at the quick-breathing boy. I was told he was doing well, considering, and I tried to pass this qualified optimism on to my drugged and anxious wife. Every hurrying footstep past the ward to the nursery next door turned her heavy-lidded green eyes in that direction. She'd seen him and she loved him—it was simple as that. I knew the strong maternal instinct in my wife, which now prevailed over sentiment or self-pity. She was desire for him to live personified.

I nearly always forget the traditional things on such occasions. I can be forgiven, perhaps. When the prospect was fairly bright, I finally thought of flowers, about mid-afternoon, but the florist had no imported Australian flowers, as they had all been taken for a wedding. I scrounged some specimens from a couple of gardens and took the limp bouquet to the hospital. Tropical flowers always flop when picked.

When I arrived at the hospital, there were the sounds of feet running, and five doctor and nurse figures were bent over the incubator. Suzanne still hadn't slept and was puffy-eyed from crying. Adam's respiratory system just wasn't up to the task, and just sixteen short hours after his birth, he died.

I prayed again in sorrow and in resignation. I also prayed in thanks that he hadn't survived longer only to go, adding the rider that I wished he hadn't lived long enough for us to know him, but I wasn't sure about that wish. You so quickly invested that bruised head with character as he lay behind the glass, his fingers spread, his legs half tucked up, a tube in his nose, his chest so small next to his head but pumping away—bravely, you reflected falsely to yourself.

When it was over, it was I who had to be brave, to make the necessary arrangements and think of things to say to help make it acceptable to Suzanne. The priest tried with the "angel in Heaven" bit. I knew there was really only myself who could find something beyond such ideas or beliefs that might help, hard as they were to grasp or to believe in the way they were meant.

Compensation finally lay in Suzanne's fertile body, and Jason was born hardly a year later.

It has been twenty-nine years since Adam died, but we still feel the loss acutely. Having Jason afterwards was wonderful, as it helped us both look forward, but Suzanne regrets the protectiveness shown to her during that traumatic time. She was not allowed to see Adam after he died, to say goodbye, and she was not present at his funeral. The lack of understanding by others remains with her and remains a regret for us both.

CRAIG'S STORY

MY WIFE, Michelle, and I had our first baby, Nathan, in 1993. Michelle had had diabetes from week thirty-two and had therefore been in and out of the hospital. Our son was born three weeks early, but everything was fine, and we went home a family.

In 1995, little knowing the heartbreak that lay in store for us, we decided to try for another baby. Within two months we were pregnant again, and we were ecstatic. Michelle had to be closely monitored because of the diabetes, but at eleven weeks an ultrasound scan told us that all was well with the pregnancy. The heartbeat was strong and the baby was growing well. We walked out of the hospital smiling, both excited and looking forward to the day our second child would be born. It would never happen.

Three weeks later, while I was washing up, I suddenly heard Michelle scream, "I'm bleeding, I'm bleeding!" My whole world just turned upside down.

We called the hospital but were told there was nothing they could do. Michelle was told that she should go to bed and stay there until the bleeding stopped. When it didn't stop, we ignored their advice and I drove her to the nearby hospital, where we were forced to wait for three hours before a doctor saw us. We were told, quite simply, that our baby had probably died and that she would have to wait until the following day, Monday, before anything more could be done for her.

I prayed so much to God that day, asking that everything would be all right. What, I asked, would we tell Nathan? One moment he was going to be a big brother and the next—nothing.

When Monday finally came, Michelle was taken for another ultrasound, and from the moment I looked into the technician's eyes I knew. There was no heartbeat, but she wouldn't give us the news herself; we had to see our own doctor, who told us our baby had indeed died and arranged for Michelle to go into the hospital again for a dilation and curettage.

It was a cold, rainy winter's day when we arrived at the hospital and I watched Michelle's heart break. I just wanted to hold her and never let her go again. I wanted to try and wipe out all of her pain, but I couldn't, because at the same time my own heart had also broken. If I could have done so, I would have taken her in my arms, driven her home, and made everything all right again. This was the kind of thing that happened to other people, not to us. How could this be happening to us?

When it was all over and we finally went home, the house felt so cold. It's hard to describe, but it simply felt strange. We were each grieving in our own way, and for Michelle the hurt was so deep, even my attempts to talk to her and cuddle her were not enough.

Looking back, I believe that very few people understood my feelings about having lost our child. I wanted to cry, and I wanted someone to sit down with me and talk about how I was feeling, someone who would listen and not offer words of comfort that didn't comfort at all. If I had a dollar for every time someone has told us that it was God's way, I'd be wealthy, but instead I could just scream.

As a man, I would have liked another man, a friend, to sit with me and listen to what it felt like being the father in these circumstances, but it never happened. It's not the male way—you've got to be tough and get on with things. At the time, I found it hard to understand how everyone seemed able to carry on with their lives when we had just lost our baby, a baby who was going to join our lives. Even today, I remain angry at the lack of understanding by others of the extent of our loss.

Something remained missing from our family—for Michelle, for Nathan, and for me. It was not until August 29, 1997, that I finally saw the smile return to Michelle's face. No child would ever replace the baby we had lost, but we now had a beautiful daughter, Tara.

I love my wife for all the things she does as a mother, and I thank my lucky stars that I was given a chance to love these special gifts from God—our children. To this day I think about our little person whom we never got to hold, but I believe that one day, when my time is up, I will meet our child.

Nor should we forget the grandparents, as they too have built up expectations of involvement in a baby's life, which can no longer be fulfilled when miscarriage occurs. I look back on the time when we had our twins and my heart aches with the many regrets I have, the many things I feel I did wrong or could have done differently. We were living several hours' journey away from my parents, and we made the decision not to ask them to come to the funeral. Instead, on a cold, miserable day, Peter and I went to the cemetery alone, and we sat in our private misery as the priest laid our children to rest with words of comfort. Not understanding the full extent of my own grief, I had absolutely no idea how my parents were feeling; it simply didn't occur to me that this was their loss too.

If, through sharing what I see as my mistakes with others, just one person can avoid the same lifelong regret, then maybe my own regrets will be worthwhile. For that reason I have included my mother's, my father's, and my friend's stories. I've learned now that there's a wrong way and a right way.

MY MOTHER MARGARET'S STORY

AFTER READING the draft of this book, written by my beloved youngest daughter, I closed my eyes. What I had read enabled me to understand her better, to understand the profound effect the death of her babies has had on her as a woman, a mother, a daughter, a wife, and a friend. It also allowed me to embark on a journey in which memories of long ago came flooding back as the years slipped past in my mind.

The first window in my memory was of myself as a young and rather naive eighteen-year-old who married a handsome young army officer, reveling in all the hopes and dreams the romance promised. It was in the days before the Pill had become available, and as I was a Catholic, it was unsurprising that within a very short time I found myself pregnant. Sadly, when I was only seven months pregnant, I went into premature labor and the medical staff could do nothing to stop it. I was small-boned, and labor was difficult. It lasted for nearly three days, during which time my protests of pain were met by simple and uncompassionate statements such as, "Catholic girls don't cry!"

Finally, on Christmas Day, 1957, a tiny baby girl weighing only two and a half pounds was born. As the nurse examined me following the birth, she noticed that my stomach was still rather hard. She listened with a fetal stethoscope and merely said, "There's another baby here." I was amazed and excited, as no one had known I was carrying twins—the ultrasound, like the Pill, was not yet available, and even my large belly had not hinted at this possibility.

Twenty minutes after the birth of my first daughter, another little girl was born, only she was smaller and weaker than the first. Within twenty-four short hours, she had died. I never knew she was coming, and I was left with the one child I'd expected, but not knowing whether she too would be taken from us. Ultimately, she gained strength, and we were allowed to take her home with us. Today she is a beautiful and successful woman who is a source of great pride for me.

So many years ago, the death of a baby was not dealt with as it is today. My second daughter was taken away, and while I lay in the hospital, my husband, who is ten years older, arranged for her funeral, which he attended alone wearing a black armband. For my part, I was considered lucky, as one child had survived. I was told not to cry, and I never did.

The second window in my memory was of a time thirty years later, when my daughter lost her twins. She had told me many times during that pregnancy that she felt it wasn't right, and on each occasion I had tried to console her, hoping against hope that she was wrong. Then one day, when I was out with a friend, I suddenly felt in my heart that she was in trouble. Somehow I managed to find out that she had been taken in to her local hospital and to find Peter and speak to him. Adrienne had gone into labor and her babies were going to be born too early.

Within a few hours, she had given birth to her first son and daughter, and shortly afterwards they died. The grief I experienced that time, twelve years ago, was so great and so intense it overwhelmed me. I found myself crying for her loss and crying, at last, for my own. It was a grief that should have been dealt with decades ago, and one that made me realize the process of mourning should not be suppressed; it should be traveled through in whatever way individuals believe will help them come to terms with their loss. I, like many other women whose babies died so long ago, kept a "stiff upper lip" and moved on with my life.

I hope that, in writing this book, my darling daughter's heart has been repaired, and I hope the same for all the other people who have contributed their own sad experiences. Our sense of loss will always be there, but life goes on, and perhaps good things will come from the despair of yesteryear.

MY FATHER MICHAEL'S STORY

"REAL" MEN don't cry, and therefore they don't grieve—or so some assume. In reality, we do both and often in a more corrosive way, as so much of our hurt is internalized and suppressed.

I remember, as Margaret does, the shock of learning that she had given birth to twins, the waking of good friends, the race to the hospital, the joy at seeing our firstborn, and then the terrible heartbreaking pain on being told that her little sister had died. It was for such a pointless and senseless reason, too. Yes, she was premature, but her identical twin managed to survive where she didn't. And the reason? Her tiny lungs were filled with mucus, and the hospital, those forty-two years ago in the middle of Africa, did not have the equipment necessary to clear them. I blamed them then and I blame them now for not being able to save my child, and although I know it is unreasonable for me to do so, I just can't help it.

So Noelle was lost and Carolyn lives, but we are, as Margaret says, immensely proud of her. Sadly, though, in all those long years since her birth, I have never once spoken to her or thought of her without knowing that she should be two, and I weep inside at the abysmal cruelty of a fate that has condemned Carolyn to a lifetime deprived of her other half.

For one of my other daughters to then have to endure the same awful tragedy years later was a doubly tragic blow. Now not the father but the grandfather, the sorrow is no less, and I mourn for my dead grandchildren as I did for my own lost daughter, the more so, perhaps, because of the devastating effect the loss of their twins has had on Adrienne and Peter. All parents know that to be helpless to prevent one's child being hurt is a thousand times worse than being hurt oneself.

Fortunately for Adrienne and Peter and for Margaret and me, other children came along who might never have been born had their older siblings lived. What I am certain of, however, is that our very much loved granddaughters will prove as much a source of love, comfort, and pride to their parents as our own daughters have proved to be for us.

IAN'S STORY

No sooner had we decided to start a family than my wife, Trish, was pregnant. It was what we had wanted from the time we first met, aged seventeen, and now the world seemed perfect: we were going to have our baby. Sadly, it was not to be, and at six weeks we discovered it was an ectopic pregnancy and Trish miscarried. We were both devastated—and amazed that so few people seemed to take our loss seriously, telling us it was a common occurrence, that it often happens with the first one.

The following three pregnancies again ended in miscarriage and tragically also resulted in the loss of both of Trish's fallopian tubes. I shall always remember the explanation of my options: a hurried sketch of the female reproductive organs on a bit of scrap paper. We became what the medical profession refers to as "an infertile couple." With that knowledge, we embarked on the long and often painful journey into the world of in vitro fertilization (IVF). It was still relatively early days for this incredible marvel of medical science, and the treatment of patients reflected this lack of experience. I still remember quite vividly sitting in the corridor of a major hospital with a number held tightly in my hand, waiting to be called, while Trish struggled on painfully with a full bladder. After five unsuccessful attempts, we filed for adoption.

As we went through the process of writing our life histories for the adoption papers, we by chance watched a couple of films that together aroused our parental instincts more than we could ever have imagined. We decided to give in vitro fertilization one more shot, and we struck it lucky; the flutter of that tiny little heartbeat on the monitor in front of us was just too much, and even the doctor was misty. It had all been worthwhile; we were going to have a baby at last.

Apart from us, the two people most elated by the news were Trish's parents, Mary and Tony. They had experienced difficulties themselves and had lost babies in the days when couples had no choice but to simply bear it and get on with life. When we were past the "initial danger period," we felt justified in making plans, and, of course, the grandparents-to-be were involved; they were supportive in the way only those who have experienced the loss of a child themselves can be—no fuss, no bother, just there.

Like every crisis I can remember, the problem struck in the middle of the night. A very quick drive to the hospital ensued, and thirty hours later our dreams were shattered; our baby was dead. Apart from feelings of hopelessness, anger, frustration, and disbelief, I was then faced with the prospect of having to tell Tony and Mary, and I knew that they too would be devastated. They were fantastic. They hid their own disappointment and gave us what we needed. They held our tiny little boy in their hands, and Heaven knows the memories that must have aroused, but they helped us through our worst nightmare.

As James had been born one day short of the required age for being legally acknowledged, any funeral arrangements were left for us to organize. I was in no fit state to do anything, so I asked Tony if he could arrange a little coffin for James, who, we had decided, would be buried in our garden. He deserved something special, and obviously Tony understood that, because he returned only about twelve hours later carrying a tiny little box. The box had been lovingly crafted with his own hands. It had chamfered edges and a specially designed fastening device for the lid so that

I wouldn't have to hammer in nails. Mary had lined the box with blue material and had made a pillow and a padded base. It was quite beautiful and far beyond our expectations.

As I lowered the handmade box containing our son into the grave beneath the tree I had given Trish for our first wedding anniversary, I couldn't help thinking how many babies there must be all over the world, from all these years, in tiny boxes, just like James.

A Hard Call

Day after day the same thought keeps
Running through my head
Is this child we are having still alive, or is this
Child dead?
It's a hard call to answer as the hope of life starts
To go numb
I am like a ship tossed at sea but calm
In the eye of the storm.

As miscarriage came, God did reclaim the life of our
Child unborn
Grief for the life in a womb and a tomb
Brief the time it was there
The gift in our heart will never depart
That's a blessing that we share.

(BY PAUL, IN MEMORY OF MONICA SINEAD)

Genetic and Chromosomal Disorders

*W*HY DID IT HAPPEN TO ME? THAT'S THE question most of us ask ourselves when we are left with empty arms and shattered dreams. But despite the frequency of miscarriage and stillbirth, it appears to be an incredibly difficult question for the medical professionals to answer.

After my first early miscarriage, I was prepared to accept the usual platitudes they sent in my direction: "It's common with the first;" "There was obviously a problem;" "It's very common in the first pregnancy when the mother has taken the Pill." And so they went on—no big deal, apparently. And anyway, I was pregnant again so soon afterwards that I didn't leave myself time to dwell on why it had happened. I tucked the experience away in my subconscious and moved on.

Twelve weeks into my twin pregnancy, I started to feel an uncomfortable tightening of my womb. I was told that Braxton Hicks's—the initial contractions—usually start only late in the third trimester, but it seemed that only I was concerned that mine had started in the first. I became increasingly aware of every twitch and every twinge, and I even began to keep a diary of how I was feeling on a day-to-day basis. My obstetrician pandered to my apparent paranoia by agreeing to frequent checkups and eventually admitting me to the hospital for a couple of days. I was monitored during my time in the hospital, but nothing constructive was ever done to alleviate the contractions.

It was only after I'd given birth that they decided I might have a problem with an irritable uterus and an incompetent cervix. These were the problems they addressed with my subsequent pregnancies by putting me on four-hourly doses of a muscle-relaxant drug and stitching my cervix. The drug was horrendous; with every dose I became quite incapable of functioning normally, as shudders coursed through my body, my hands shook uncontrollably, and the sound of my pulse deafened my ears. But, together with the stitch, it must have worked, because with both my daughters it was only when they stopped the drug and removed the stitch that the girls came rushing into the world—both four weeks before their due date.

So, with hindsight, I can look back on my twin pregnancy and ask the usual question, Why did it happen to me? And when I ask myself that, my anger returns, because I think, Surely I wasn't the only woman in the world who started to have contractions so early in pregnancy. Surely those contractions were a sign of something going on, and surely the doctors, with all their experience, must have been able to take an educated guess as to what that something was.

In the end, they did something in my subsequent pregnancies, and I was able to stay pregnant long enough for my daughters to be born with more than a fighting chance, but it wasn't soon enough for my other babies.

SHARYN'S STORY

WHEN MY husband, Peter, and I married in July 1997, we were ready to start a family. Having children has always been something I knew I would do one day, because, having been raised in a close and loving family, I felt it was important and special. My expectations, however, were quite realistic, as my own parents had had some difficulty starting a family, and as children we were aware that having a baby is a precious and wonderful thing that cannot be taken for granted.

With my usual vigor, I researched and planned the whole process thoroughly. This involved reading a lot of books, magazines, and publications on the Internet. I was very excited about the thought of having a baby, but at the back of my mind I also worried that we might have some problems. Over a period of a few months, however, my fears and apprehension gave way to a quiet confidence that seemed to come from what I can only describe as my inner self. Without understanding how, I seemed to know that everything was going to be fine.

In December 1998, Pete and I began trying for a baby, and to our delight I became pregnant the first month. I can't describe how happy we were and how relieved I was to find out that at least we could conceive a child. As the excitement built, we began to keep a diary and to take photographs to track my changing body. Looking back, the plans Pete and I made for the baby and the endless things we discussed in that first month were amazing. Needless to say, we couldn't keep the news to ourselves, and by the time I had reached the eight-week mark we had told most of our family and friends the news.

Then, at only nine weeks, I had a miscarriage. It was a blighted ovum, where the egg had been fertilized but had then failed to develop. My reaction was one of utter shock when I found myself being referred to a specialist for a dilation and curettage the following day. As a range of emotions began to invade my senses, the tears began, yet I was oblivious of what was still to come. In the hospital we saw a doctor who, with great sensitivity, explained the facts and gently spoke to us about the emotional impact of miscarriage. He told us that the enormity of what had happened would not hit us until later, and he explained how other people, both family and friends, might not react as we would want them to. So much of what he said helped us deal with our grief, and I shall always be grateful to him for that.

Sadly, he also told us that the ultrasound that had identified the blighted ovum also showed evidence of a disease called trophoblastic disease. Essentially, this means that at fertilization, when the egg and sperm join together, a healthy placenta is not formed. The ovum deteriorates, and the placental tissue invades the uterus; it is not a cancer, but it is likened to a cancer due to the nature of the cells, which multiply and have the potential to spread to other organs. Very occasionally, a molar pregnancy becomes malignant, so close medical follow-up is essential, and in my case this involved weekly blood tests to monitor the pregnancy hormone (HCG) level as it fell. We were told at the outset that the next course of action would be chemotherapy if the situation did not resolve itself.

With this particular disease, the symptoms of pregnancy become severe very early on. After the dilation and curettage those symptoms disappeared virtually overnight, leaving me with nothing, not even a slight reminder of what might have been. For that reason as much as any other, I returned to work almost immediately, expecting to be able to continue as before, albeit without the joy of impending motherhood.

Pete and I were still grieving, but we were fortunate in that we could talk to each other about our feelings. In fact, we talked a great deal about it all, and as a result, we agreed that the miscarriage had strengthened our already strong relationship. Life, it seemed, was getting back to normal.

Although I threw myself into my work, leaving little or no time to dwell on the tragedy, at 5:00 P.M. every Friday I would once again be reminded as I discussed the findings of my blood tests with my doctor. Ordinarily, it would be hoped that the HCG would drop with each passing week, thereby signaling a natural curing process. As it was, mine plateaued, meaning some microscopic cells from the diseased tissue were still in my body somewhere. Looking back, I wonder how I ever managed to progress emotionally through this period.

Once again we found ourselves facing a specialist—this time another wonderful doctor who was an expert in gynecological cancer and who explained that chemotherapy was now essential. He eased my concerns about losing my hair and explained that the course of treatment was a fairly mild form, with few or no side effects. Armed with more information, I felt some relief, and I started the chemotherapy the next day.

I launched into this new phase of treatment while at the same time arranging my professional life in such a way as to alleviate some of the pressures and responsibilities. I actually thought things were okay until suddenly, without warning, I hit rock bottom emotionally. I realized I was tired of putting on a brave face and tired of maintaining a high level of professionalism when everyone around me seemed oblivious to my pain. I couldn't face going to work anymore and having to deal with people who couldn't understand what was happening to me. Even my relationship with Pete seemed to suffer, as he didn't seem to notice what I was going through. I was emotionally bouncing off the walls.

What neither of us knew was that, although the chemotherapy appeared to have been the trigger for my feelings, it really wasn't the focus for my anguish. I took two weeks off work and explored my feelings and thoughts alone and at my own pace. I discovered that I hadn't dealt with some aspects of my grief and that I needed to be a little bit selfish. I had to focus on myself for a while in order to acknowledge my feelings and establish some peace of mind. I did this, and I'm a better person for having done so.

The chemotherapy has been successful and will continue for some time yet. I know what I experienced is rare medically; however, I don't believe that the emotions I experienced were either rare or uncommon. The unusual amount of follow-up care and treatment I received after my miscarriage prevented me from burying my feelings, and it no doubt brought the issue to a head. For that reason alone, I regard my molar pregnancy as a positive experience. I still cry, of course, but I know that it is helping me each time I do.

Sometimes I wonder why that special little soul popped into my life for such a short time; she turned my world upside down, and it was the hardest thing I've ever had to deal with. I believe, though, that how we deal with our experiences, both good and bad, is what defines us as persons. It's funny, but I still have that inner feeling of confidence that everything is going to be okay, and I can't help feeling that that little soul will be back again when the time is right.

Lynn's Story

At the age of twenty-six, I found myself pregnant for the first time. My breasts were so sore I naively went to the doctor thinking I had breast cancer, but instead I received the wonderful news of my impending motherhood.

My husband, Mark, and I were so excited as we went for my first ultrasound at eleven and a half weeks, but our excitement was to be short-lived: I had a blighted ovum, and our baby had died inside me some weeks earlier. This was to be the beginning of a long and difficult journey for us, as within a year I had two more pregnancies, both of which ended in the same tragic way.

With all the pain and grief I was experiencing, I needed, more than anything, to be treated by a doctor who could show me some measure of compassion and care. Unfortunately, the doctor I was seeing at the time seemed annoyed by what was happening to me and was extremely patronizing in the way he dealt with me. Coming to terms with the way my life had been turned upside down in such a short space of time was hard enough already, so I made the decision to change doctors. The doctor who was recommended to me was the most kind and understanding man I have ever met. At our first meeting with him, he took us into a private room and simply listened to us as we spoke about our experiences. He then examined all of my medical records and decided that if I became pregnant again I should take half an aspirin a day and a steroid called prednisone.

With new hope, Mark and I decided that we would try again, and two months later I became pregnant for the fourth time. Sadly, although I had started the medication as advised, the pregnancy ended at six weeks. This time I chose not to go into the hospital for a dilation and curettage, and instead I allowed depression to set in as I finally started to accept the fact that I might never have a baby.

This realization was possibly the hardest thing I had ever had to come to terms with, and in doing so I felt very alone in my grief. There seemed to be no one I could talk to about how I felt. Most of my friends at the time had newborn babies or infants and felt uneasy listening to my sad story, and, to make matters worse, Mark and I were fighting more and more as we each came to terms with our grief. Men deal with the situation very differently from women. They don't talk about it, and in many ways they seem to figure that once it's over, it's over. They don't seem to carry the emotional baggage in the same way women do—it's as though they can see only what is going on on the outside. When a woman is pregnant, she is pregnant, no matter how far.

Luckily, though, we saw what was happening to us and how potentially destructive the whole emotional saga was in terms of our relationship. As hard as it was, we decided to take a year off the "baby scene"; we bought a ski boat and we did things together, and it was the best year we had ever had. The stress of falling pregnant, staying pregnant, losing the baby, and recovering was all out of our lives for a time, and we lived a normal, happy, healthy year.

The following year, we sold our house and bought a six-and-a-half-acre property elsewhere, but the day we moved in, I found out that I was pregnant again, and I was devastated. As I cried, I realized that I wasn't ready to go through it all again. I wasn't ready to go back to the hospital and to start with so much hope only to have it dashed with yet another miscarriage. But I couldn't ignore what was happening to my body, so with a heavy heart I went back to my doctor and told him the news. He immediately did an ultrasound, which showed the baby was six weeks old and very much alive.

Once again, I started the medication, and the doctor agreed to a weekly ultrasound, if only to help keep my stress levels down. Seven weeks, still alive; eight weeks, still going; nine weeks, ten weeks, all the way to eighteen weeks—my baby was still alive and growing, and I could finally share some good news with our family and friends.

With so many other false starts, I tried hard to contain my excitement, but it was growing daily as my baby grew within me.

This was actually going to happen! I had reached thirty-five weeks when, without warning, the pain of labor, so often denied me in the past, began. I couldn't believe it, but there I was in the hospital with other pregnant women and the nurses telling me I would be a mommy very soon. Me, a mommy? Three days later, in the early hours of Sunday morning, Luke James came into this world weighing six pounds, three ounces. Our son!

I have since learned that I have a condition called antiphospholipid syndrome. This is a disorder of the immune system that causes blood clotting, which for me means that when the baby starts to grow, my blood clots the umbilical cord, and the baby dies. Now, if I become pregnant, I have to take aspirin and also inject myself daily with a drug called Clexane, an anticoagulant. There are never any guarantees though, and a few months ago I miscarried my fifth baby. Having my beautiful son in my arms, I was able to deal with this tragedy more easily than with the others, but the anger, pain, and grief are still there.

Mark and I would dearly love to have another baby, but for now we have decided to do what we did a few years ago and take time off. We will enjoy being a family of three, and in a year or so we'll try one more time. If it fails, well, it will be just the three of us, and that is okay. Despite everything, we consider ourselves to be the lucky ones; we succeeded, many don't.

CATHY'S STORY

MARK AND I have been married for three and a half years, and all we've ever wanted is to have a family. When I got pregnant in

1996, we were over the moon, little knowing that our future was to hold so much sadness. Soon after our lovely daughter, Hannah, was born, she was diagnosed with cystic fibrosis. The doctors told us that if I were to get pregnant again, there would be a one-in-four chance of the baby's having this illness. Hearing the terrible news about Hannah and then having to come to terms with such uncertainty was almost unbearable. All our hopes and dreams seemed to be lying shattered around us as we forced ourselves to consider the future and the possibility of never having another child.

After a great deal of soul searching, discussions, and heartache, we decided to take the chance and try again. Within a month I was pregnant and we found ourselves living with a seesaw of emotions as excitement and joy gave way to fear of what might be.

To find out what the future held for our little baby, I had a chorionic villus sampling when I was ten and a half weeks pregnant. We were told that the results would take about seven days, and in the meantime Mark and I talked endlessly about what we would do if cystic fibrosis was detected. Because this is such a terrible, life-threatening illness, we realized it would be unfair to bring a child with it into the world; we knew that we would have no choice but to end the pregnancy.

Much to our relief, it took only two days before we received the wonderful news that our baby, a little boy, was fine. Mark immediately named him Alexander, and together we started to plan for the future—everything seemed so perfect. Then, at fifteen and a half weeks, a routine ultrasound showed that Alexander had died about two weeks before. I had had no idea, no symptoms to tell me that anything was wrong.

Our lives turned upside down as Mark went on a downward spiral of depression and refused to speak to anyone—not me or his family or even his friends—and I still have days when all I want to do is cry. I didn't think that we would last the distance, but I was wrong. With a lot of love and support from each other, we are just starting to come to terms with what happened to us. We have a future.

Tricia's Story

ALEXANDER URIAH was born and died on September 13, 1997, two days before my thirty-second birthday. My husband, Wayne, and I had gone for a routine ultrasound when I was eighteen weeks pregnant, only to be told the devastating news that something was terribly wrong with our baby and further tests would be necessary.

The medical staff who dealt with us as the tests were carried out were all so kind and compassionate, but the news was not good. They told us our baby boy would not survive, as he had a condition known as posterior urethral valve. Essentially, this meant that a membrane, as thin as a piece of paper, had not separated in the urethra, resulting in a blockage. He could not pass urine, so it had built up inside his tiny body until his stomach was completely distended and his system had become poisoned by toxins—a random event, they said, with no known cause, and unlikely to occur in any subsequent pregnancy.

Our baby died the following day, but, tragically, the attempts to induce labor failed. The following day was my birthday, and my obstetrician said to me, "Birthday memories are lifetime memories. This will be a lifetime memory itself, so we want to avoid them happening on the same day." He then sent me home and told me to come back to the hospital two days later.

Again they induced labor, and this time, after five and a half hours, I gave birth to our poor baby. The medical staff were all as wonderful as they had been a few short days before, when they'd broken the terrible news to us. The midwife wrapped Alexander in a beautiful bunny blanket and left us alone to spend our last precious moments with him.

I will always remember how warm Alexander was when I held him and how cold he was when we buried him—a heartbreaking comparison. His little mouth opened while we were holding him, and it was almost too much to bear, knowing I would never feed him. He was so still as the midwife took some photos for us, wrote out a crib card, and took foot- and handprints. My deepest regret is that, although she advised us to take photographs of our own, my husband thought it was better not to. To this day I wish he had thought differently.

As our baby was less than twenty weeks old, he could not be issued a birth certificate, and without one no official gravestone or marker in a cemetery was possible. This is something I still find extremely hard to cope with, and had I known about it, I would have held on to my baby for as long as my body allowed, hoping that he might make it to twenty weeks.

We were fortunate, however, that our minister allowed us to bury Alexander in an unmarked grave in the children's section of the cemetery; I could not have left our precious baby to be "put out" with the hospital waste. The minister read some prayers—some have recently been written for the unborn—and gave Alexander a Christian burial, asking my husband at the end to help fill in the grave. We asked only close family to come to the funeral, and among them was our fourteen-year-old niece, who wrote a very moving and special poem, and our eight-year-old nephew, who made an everlasting flower that was buried with our baby.

Throughout the whole experience, we felt our attitude helped us to cope. Many people say, Why us? but we said, Why not us? There is nothing that sets us apart from other people, that makes us exempt from misfortune. I feel there is a sisterhood among those of us who have lost babies—it is an invisible bond of support. The grieving is never over, and there is always an ache in your heart and soul for your lost baby.

On July 28, 1998, I gave birth to a healthy little boy, Liam Alexander Uriah. Although we were given the opportunity of knowing the sex of our baby before he was born, we chose not to know. The health of the baby was what mattered most to us, and we got our wish: a healthy child. We are blessed.

NICOLE'S STORY

WHEN MY husband, David, and I decided it was time to begin our family, we planned the pregnancy to coincide with the school summer holidays so it would not disrupt the school year. We were fortunate to get pregnant quickly, and our baby was due on January 2, which also happened to be our third wedding anniversary. We were thrilled and excited, as well as a little apprehensive about the prospect of becoming parents.

Then, when I was seven weeks pregnant, I began to bleed, and even though I rested and prayed, we lost the baby. It was so sad and terrifying at the same time; in a way it was as if it were happening to someone else. Our family and the few close friends we had told were supportive, but there's no doubt it was difficult for them to understand the significance of our loss.

Despite our pain, we were confident enough to try again, believing it couldn't happen to anyone twice. Nevertheless, when I became pregnant once more, the excitement was tinged with fear that it just might happen again.

I passed the seven-week stage with relief and started to grow in confidence that this time our baby would stay with us. At nine weeks the bleeding started, and, absolutely terrified but under doctor's orders, I stayed in bed for two days. Nothing, though, could stop a second miscarriage, and early one morning my husband rushed me to the hospital, where my obstetrician bluntly told me what I already knew—my baby had died. Our second baby was gone and I felt like a failure. I just remember crying from so deep within my heart, grieving for our two babies whom I never got to meet or hold, and in fear of never being a mother. I was racked with guilt; should I have rested more, should I have done less housework, worried less, eaten more?

I cried also for the insensitivity of other people. Our families felt the loss too, but friends either made hurtful comments like, "Nicole, what are you doing wrong?" or, worse, they said nothing at all. The saddest moments for us were when our friends did not even acknowledge our loss. A simple "I'm sorry about the baby" would have sufficed.

Although reluctant, I agreed to undergo a series of blood tests in an effort to discover why I suffered recurrent miscarriages. After six anxious weeks, it was discovered that indeed we did have a problem, but, unfortunately, it was not something that could be fixed by any form of medical intervention. I have a balanced translocation, the bottom line being that with any pregnancy I have only a 50 percent chance of carrying my baby to full term. We looked on the news positively, and we were grateful to the two wonderful genetic counselors we saw at Westmead Hospital. They were the first two medical people who had offered us support and sympathy, and they remained positive about our prospects for parenthood.

David and I were blessed, as I became pregnant within a month of meeting with the counselors, and in July 1997, we had a healthy nine-pound boy whom we named Gerard Patrick. Surviving my third pregnancy was made easier by the love and support I received from family and close friends. Also, as I had found my original obstetrician to be lacking in his ability to show compassion, I moved under the care of another one. I found him to be kind, gentle, and very positive and supportive throughout my pregnancy. The first three months had been extremely difficult, as every twinge brought with it fresh fears for my third child's survival.

Now we find that, as our son approaches his second birthday, we long for another child, and already we have had a third miscarriage. The sadness of nearly three years ago still comes to haunt us as memories resurface from time to time, and I cry for the children we have loved and lost. However, we live in hope; we know I can carry a baby to full term, it's just that God is waiting for the right time.

Current research argues for the primary reason for miscarriage, still-birth, and neonatal death being a genetic abnormality in the baby or chromosomal problems in either parent. The fact remains that there are really so many causes of this tragedy. More often than not, a woman will miscarry or the baby will die later in pregnancy without anyone knowing the reasons why. However, once these factors are identified, there is at least some hope in subsequent pregnancies, as the mother and baby will be monitored more closely. It also undoubtedly helps the parents to have an explanation for what has happened; few of us would deny the emotional impact when no explanation is forthcoming. That is not, of course, to say that the grief itself is lessened, but merely that some modicum of comfort can be found in the knowledge of why our babies died.

The detection of a genetic abnormality or chromosomal problem during a pregnancy can place the parents in a situation requiring inordinate strength. Having to choose between ending a pregnancy where there is little or no chance of the baby's surviving after birth or continuing with the knowledge that the child's quality of life will be very poor even if he or she does survive brings with it a whole new set of problems.

It is absolutely normal, in the euphoria of pregnancy and all it promises for the future, for women to occasionally fear the possibility of their children being less than perfect. Will they have all their fingers and toes? Will they have a disfigurement or a mental deficiency? These are natural questions we all ask ourselves and then usually dismiss, preferring to move on to happier and more positive thoughts of the child we are nurturing. But there are some couples for whom these fears become a reality. Having acquiesced to routine tests during the *pregnancy, they suddenly find themselves facing a doctor whose words turn their world upside down. When a baby dies naturally, it is hard enough to accept, but when the parents are faced with having to terminate the pregnancy because of severe problems with the baby, there are elements to their grief over and above those of other parents'—not the least being that other people may not understand their lack of choice in the matter.*

There can be a multitude of reasons for terminating a pregnancy but in the case of miscarriage, abortion has its own aura of taboo. Whatever the reason for the termination, women are not encouraged to express their emotions and cannot, therefore, find understanding from others at a time when it is most needed. In the following stories we hear from women who have come to an understanding of the whys involved with their loss, and some very brave women share with us their turmoil when confronted with the difficult decision to terminate their pregnancy.

Ros's Story

I'VE LOST five babies, five separate pregnancies, all quite early on, but with each new one came the familiar feelings of excitement and a new hope for the future. With my third pregnancy, I had reached seventeen and a half weeks, and everything seemed great. I was so happy, I felt good, and I was so pleased, because with this pregnancy I'd grown bigger more quickly. I looked pregnant and I felt pregnant.

Weeks earlier, I'd had a chorionic villus sampling for chromosomal defects and had been assured that my baby, a little boy whom I named Rafael, was absolutely fine. Hence I lay there happily, enjoying an apparently routine ultrasound, listening to the radiologist telling me that the baby's heartbeat was strong and pointing out his head and arms.

Suddenly, silence filled the room, and in an instant my world turned upside down. That moment of silence following the almost imperceptible intake of breath by the radiologist as she scans your pregnant belly stays with you forever. Until that moment you have been a happy, expectant mother with nothing more important to look forward to than the wonderful experience of giving birth to your first child. Any woman who has been through a similar experience will understand the horror of the moment when you realize that something is very wrong but you are made to wait for confirmation. In my case, the radiologist refused to say anything and instead led me to a private room furnished with little more than a box of tissues and told me to wait for my obstetrician. My partner was called, but meanwhile I sat weak-kneed, trembling, and almost incoherent, feeling as though I'd just been in an accident.

When the doctor finally arrived, he told me that Rafael had Potter's syndrome; there was no amniotic fluid, his kidneys were covered in cysts, he had no anus, and there were a multitude of other problems previous tests had failed to pick up on. The doctor explained that my baby boy had no chance of survival outside the womb and there was no alternative, therefore, but to terminate the pregnancy immediately.

It was so hard to accept that this life inside me was doomed, and it was made more shocking because they didn't give me any alternative and they didn't counsel me at all. I've found that a lot of doctors don't seem to be logical and therefore they are incapable of the compassion necessary in these situations.

In desperation, I asked if we could operate on the cysts, but it was explained that Rafael's jaw wasn't properly developed, and with no fluid in the womb he hadn't learned to swallow. Even if I went ahead with the pregnancy, I would undoubtedly have a stillbirth.

I felt suicidal as, two days later, I made my way to the hospital. I walked out across the road without looking, and my partner said to me, "What are you doing—why are you walking across the road like that?" All I said was that I really didn't care.

Once I'd been admitted, they began the process of inducing labor. For three days I lay there, for the most part alone, as my partner and I were not getting on well at the time, and waited. A whole spectrum of people seemed to come in and out: medical staff, social workers, and others, both good and bad. It just wasn't consistent, and they seemed completely oblivious to my grief and anguish. With the exception of one nurse, they did little more for me than give me a small white pail, which they left on the shelf beside me. There was no explanation. I just kept looking at this pail, knowing it was there for them to take away what finally would remain of my precious baby. When Rafael was born, I was alone and frightened. I was on the toilet, and I found myself reluctant to look down at him, believing the image would be so horrifying it would remain engraved in my mind forever.

As difficult as it was, I could face the fact that my darling son had died, and, in a way, all I wanted was to get it over with and to get on with the next pregnancy. But at the same time I was feeling like a traitor, as if somehow I was killing my own child, even though I had no choice at all. To make matters worse, the placenta, which was badly shredded, didn't entirely expel, and the obstetrician said I would need to have a curettage to take out the rest. I couldn't bear the thought of going through anymore, so I chose not to have the operation, and instead I simply went home to grieve. Unfortunately, I ended up hemorrhaging and was rushed back into the hospital, only to find myself in the same bed where I'd lost the baby. It was unbelievably sad and incredibly traumatic.

Afterwards, although the hospital offered the services of a funeral director, it was the laws of the Jewish religion that dictated what happened to Rafael. Judaism does not acknowledge a baby born in those circumstances as a person; a burial follows a life, and life starts only when the baby has taken its first breath. Instead, as an outlet for my grief, I had a small service with a wonderful rabbi. Subsequently, I've planted trees in Israel in Rafael's memory, and I've dedicated prayer books to him. I'm guided by my religion, and the belief that a life doesn't exist without a reason in some ways makes it easier for me to accept what happened.

At the time, most people didn't know what to say to me. A lot of people I worked with, when they found out what had happened, didn't call. When I asked them why they hadn't, even though they were supposed to be really good friends, their response was simply that they didn't know what to say to me. I realized it was the women who had children of their own who were more inclined to come up to me and give me a hug. People, I believe, expect you to grieve, but they don't expect you to grieve for more than a couple of weeks.

When your baby dies, you know no better, and few, if any, people can offer advice about what to do in order to lessen the regrets that inevitably engulf you later. I never held Rafael, but my regret at not having done so has undoubtedly been lessened because of the kindness shown by a wonderful nurse named Carol. She gently laid him in a bed, covered his tiny body with a sheet, laid a flower next to his head, and took some photographs—a simple but compassionate act that gave me the gift of precious, tangible memories of my son.

In return, I gave her a delicate necklace I'd only recently bought, so that she might also remember Rafael with something beautiful. Last year she wrote to me after seeing my name in a newspaper; she said she still had the necklace, she still remembered Rafael, and she just wanted to know if I'd ever had a baby. That was such a wonderful thing to happen.

I wanted so much to have a child that, despite all the pain and grief, I was determined to get pregnant again. The problems I'd had with the placenta during Rafael's birth meant it wasn't easy, and sadly, when I did manage to get pregnant again, I had a blighted ovum—a pregnancy without staying power.

There were no investigations into why I'd had so many miscarriages. They simply told me it was one of those things because I'd started my journey into motherhood so late in life. It's a life choice that so many women make today, but one awful doctor saw it as his right to lecture me on the issue of women trying to get pregnant too old. Nevertheless, he conducted a test that showed one of my ovaries wasn't working. He expected me to have been told this before, but no one had ever thought to do so.

Eventually, however, in spite of everything, I became pregnant again. With this pregnancy I had an amniocentesis, but I didn't know, if the results had been bad, whether or not I could have elected to go through that again. Isn't it cruel? It's just so cruel.

I went through the pregnancy being so scared the whole time. The birth was easy, but I had an epidural, and they had to use forceps; in the end they pulled him out. Later in the day they put him in an incubator and then took him into special care because I had noticed that he wasn't sucking well. But when I went in to see him, I freaked out, because every conceivable part of him seemed to have tubes and things attached. This most terrible doctor said he wasn't worried, as the baby wasn't going to die right now, although he might die later.

They started to do some tests, but I really wanted to have him with me, so they took out all the tubes and allowed me to hold him. With their permission I took him back with me into the mothers' room, and eventually everyone else left and it was just the two of us. I wanted to try and feed him on my own now, and I think that, as they'd given him a drip, it actually gave him the energy to be able to suck. At that point I held him, and looking into his eyes, I knew that this child was going to be okay. I took him back to the ward with me and I lay down in the bed with him—he was all right.

I think in some ways it can be harder for the parent when the new baby is the same sex as the child who's died. I was fortunate to have a friend with me at the time of Joel's birth. She's very spiritual, and she said she could feel that this new child was not Rafael. "He's not Rafael," she kept saying. Her words offered both comfort and relief, and I was able to move on in my new life with Joel unhindered.

Basically, I haven't spoken publicly about my experiences before, as I think people would have been embarrassed to read about it. It's so personal and so deep; I don't think people feel quite right having what they see as an unacceptable amount of emotional and personal knowledge about another person. But I'm happy for this to be public now, because time has passed, and now that I have a son, they can see I'm not a completely sad case. Life has gone on, and I think it's important that people can see another side of me—see that I'm not just this very tough person, I have been through something in my life.

I would still love another baby, even now. I think that giving birth is the most fantastic thing a woman can do, the most wonderful thing she can experience. I haven't tried to get pregnant again since then, and I've probably left it till too late, but there's so much going on in my life—looking after my son being the most important thing—that I don't really tend to dwell on the past.

Rafael remains a part of my life, and I share his memory with my beautiful son Joel, who is now five years old. I've shown the photos Carol took of Rafael to a few very close friends, and I've made a point of telling Joel that he does have an older brother. When we were at the hospital memorial service, they gave us a plant cutting. It's now a big bush, and when Joel and I look at it, we're looking at Rafael—I call the bush Rafael.

For me, when a baby dies, it is like going through fire and coming out again on the other side. Rafael's death was the most difficult experience of my life; there's no doubt that it changed me as a person, but I have learned so much from it. I have found an inner strength I never knew I had, and, more important, I have learned how much to value the gift of life.

Joanne's Story

AFTER SEVEN years of marriage, my husband and I decided it was time to start a family. We were fortunate, and I got pregnant without difficulty and had a wonderful pregnancy until I reached twenty-six weeks. I was fit and healthy, but I really wanted an ultrasound, so at my insistence my doctor organized one for us.

Few people go into these things believing they'll be told anything other than how well the baby is growing, that he or she has all his or her fingers and toes, and, if you ask, what sex the baby is. As I lay there with those same expectations, I realized that the nurse seemed to be uneasy talking about what we were seeing on the screen. We had to prompt her to show us our baby's heartbeat, arms, and legs. We wanted to be reassured, but that reassurance wasn't forthcoming—instead she seemed preoccupied with measuring the baby and collecting data.

Our growing fear was compounded when we were told to wait and were then told by a doctor to discuss the findings of the ultrasound with our obstetrician immediately. The urgency with which he expressed this need and the lack of any other information meant that my husband and I spent a traumatic twenty-four hours as we tried unsuccessfully to reach our doctor. Things always seem worse at night, and that evening, although my husband tried desperately to give me some reassurance that all was fine, we both knew that it wasn't.

The next morning I had to work, but, desperate to know what was happening to the child inside me, I called the doctor and insisted that he give me the results over the phone. I was stunned when he told me our baby had Potter's syndrome and was not going to live. One of my colleagues drove me home, and my immediate reaction was to put away everything that I had carefully laid out in the nursery. I just wanted to distance myself from the baby and from the hurt.

Potter's syndrome is an extremely rare genetic disorder that affects only male children; the kidneys form cysts and therefore cannot function. Our doctor explained the implications of Potter's to us and then went on, to our utter incredulity, to ask us whether we wanted to induce labor or carry the baby to full term. I couldn't believe what he was saying. He appeared to be offering us a choice, but ultimately there was no hope of saving our son, so what choice was there? I kept thinking, Is this really happening to me? Why me?

My husband and I went home that Friday and spent a horrific weekend in the knowledge that the child I was carrying was going to die. On the Monday, with a heavy heart, I went into the hospital, where they began the process of inducing labor. I gave birth to a beautiful little boy who weighed one pound, twelve ounces. We named him Justin, and during the short time we had with him, my husband took photographs of us together. I can remember saying that he was cold and wrapping him up in the little blanket. Then they took him away.

Justin would be eight years old now. My husband and I still talk about what it would have been like to have him here with us, but we have since been blessed with two beautiful daughters, Paige and Brittany.

One day I hope a test will be developed to detect Potter's syndrome at a much earlier stage in pregnancy.

FIONA'S STORY

MY EXPERIENCES have covered a period of ten years. My first daughter was conceived and born with no difficulty. After nine months of trying for a second baby, I finally became pregnant again, only to lose the baby at seven weeks. We got on with our lives that time, thinking I would soon become pregnant again. But how wrong we were.

It took eighteen months before I was finally pregnant again. Then, at seven weeks, the spotting began, and as many women who have had a miscarriage know, when you see that blood, it is like the end of the world. An ultrasound showed the baby to have a healthy heartbeat, but the bleeding continued, and somehow the pregnancy simply didn't feel right.

My visits to the doctor had been met with her impatience. She told me it was a common occurrence and that I should put up with it. Eventually, though, when I was twelve weeks pregnant, my concerns became so great I pleaded with her to do another ultrasound. She reluctantly agreed to do one, and they found that my baby had died three weeks earlier. With no support or counseling, I was sent home to wonder why this kept happening to me. What had I done when I'd had a perfectly normal pregnancy with my first daughter?

After so many miscarriages, and with so many questions raging through my head, I demanded that tests be carried out. The answer was devastating: I had a translocated X chromosome. There was a 50 percent chance that with any boy I conceived either I would miscarry or the baby would be born severely retarded, mentally and physically.

We so desperately wanted more children that, despite the risks and with the help of fertility drugs, I became pregnant again. This time I was pregnant with twins. The pregnancy was fraught with anxiety as we waited endlessly for the results of tests, each time hoping and praying that everything would be all right. Finally, I gave birth to a healthy boy and girl, and we were ecstatic.

Maybe we were greedy wanting more children, but three years ago I became pregnant again, and, sadly, the worst was to come. Again the spotting started, again I tried to toughen myself for what I believed was the inevitable, and eventually, at twelve weeks, I miscarried another set of twins. How much mental agony can a woman take? Physically it was all over in a day or so, but mentally the scars remain.

Finally, in July 1998, at thirty-six years of age, I became pregnant for the last time. Once again I started to bleed, but an ultrasound showed everything to be normal, and at seven weeks the bleeding ceased. Our hopes soared. Then, at eleven weeks, I had a chorionic villus sampling, and the results showed our baby boy had Klinefelter's syndrome—instead of XY chromosomes, he had XXY. The doctors told us in no uncertain terms that the baby would either die at birth or be severely retarded, so at fifteen weeks we were left with no choice but to terminate the pregnancy.

We believe in our hearts that it was the right decision, but the grief, guilt, and emptiness I feel is incredible. I still grieve for the babies I've lost. People don't seem to understand how you can grieve for someone you've never known, but I do grieve, and I will probably continue to do so. I know I'm luckier that a lot of women who have suffered miscarriages, as I have three healthy children whom I love dearly. Miscarriage affects the whole family. My husband rarely talks about it, but I know he feels the losses as much as I do.

Whether a baby dies at six weeks or at twenty weeks, those expectations are still there, and there is always that loss of what could have been.

JOANNA'S STORY

I HAVE been pregnant four times, and two of those pregnancies have ended in miscarriage. The first was short-lived, as I miscarried at seven weeks, but as throughout those early weeks I knew there was something wrong, it was not really a surprise, just very sad. I named the baby Gabriel(le).

During my next pregnancy, miscarriage was always at the back of my mind, especially as at the start there were similar complications; I had constant bleeding and considerable pain due to a corpus luteum cyst. Generally, though, this pregnancy felt different, and in January 1995 I gave birth to William Xavier, my darling son.

It was really my third pregnancy that was the most traumatic. Once again, from the very beginning, I felt there was something wrong. I went for my routine eighteen-week ultrasound and, taking off my glasses so that I couldn't see the images of my baby, I asked the technician not to tell me the sex. The ultrasound took nearly an hour, and by then any hopes I'd clung to that everything was fine had vanished. I knew with absolute certainty that something was wrong with my baby. With this knowledge, I went to see my own doctor and waited while he went through the usual checkup items, until finally he turned to me and told me what I was waiting to hear: the ultrasound had shown the baby had a diaphragmatic hernia. Babies with a diaphragmatic hernia have an 80 percent mortality rate, and no one could find us anyone whose baby had survived, but still we were told "we had a choice" about whether we wanted me to stay pregnant.

We went home facing the worst decision of our lives. We spoke to a number of people, including a friend who is a pediatrician, and to the organization Support after Fetal Diagnosis of Abnormality (SAFDA), and we knew we had to terminate the pregnancy. In June 1996, I delivered a son, Maximillian—I can no longer refer to the birth process as labor—and legally, because I was less than twenty weeks along, he did not exist. We nevertheless chose to have him cremated and held a funeral service for him.

To get pregnant a fourth time, I required fertility drugs. As a result of the drugs, I was suffering from extremely heavy periods and generally I found myself putting other things in my life on hold, just in case. I couldn't go on like that forever, so I gave myself a deadline by which time either I would be pregnant or I would stop trying. In the last few weeks before the deadline, I finally became pregnant again, and it was the first pregnancy without pain and bleeding. Because of all that had happened in the past, we chose not to tell people I was pregnant until I had reached twenty weeks. I also totally refused all forms of tests, including blood tests and the ultrasound, and in May 1998, Eleanor Xanthe was born.

Today, when people ask me how many children I have, I always pause before answering. I have two living children, but if I say two I feel that I am ignoring my other two children, who were just as real and as much a part of me as William and Eleanor. Gabriel and Max simply never made it to full term and never had the opportunity to grow and develop as my other children have.

It Happened Today

It happened in the world today
Issues were debated
Decisions made in Parliament
Prices were inflated
The price of gold did rise and fall
Executives were stressed
Working mothers juggled
And ladies still got dressed
The ozone layer weakened, there were images from Mars
Public figures thrown from office
And drunkards thrown from bars
The planet still rotated
The coastline washed to sea
Our resources still depleted
And it didn't bother me
In a place so insignificant
Amongst the flowers I cry
A mother held her infant son
And then she said goodbye.

(BY NATALIE, IN MEMORY OF SAM DEAN ANTHONY)

The Gift of Life

*T*HERE WAS A TIME WHEN COUPLES WHO COULD NOT conceive or who suffered recurrent miscarriages or stillbirths had to stoically face the prospect that they would never be parents. With the exception of adoption, there were few, if any, alternatives left for them but to face facts and move on accordingly.

I always considered myself to be extremely fortunate in that I could get pregnant easily. Although at one point I seriously thought I might never be able to have a child, I knew that physically, at least, I could keep trying; it was a question of whether emotionally I could continue to cope with the pain. But with each loss, the desperation to have a child grew, and not knowing what the future held, at one stage we did consider adopting a baby. It was still only a matter of weeks since we'd lost the twins, but, as I say, I was desperate. For me there was an urgent, almost primal, need to become a mother, and I was prepared to do anything to meet that need.

I can still see myself with an array of names and telephone numbers spread out in front of me as I began to tentatively call around and inquire how to go about finding a baby. It didn't occur to me for a moment that we wouldn't be suitable. Here we were, a healthy, happy, well-adjusted, well-educated, and financially secure couple with a great deal of love to give—why wouldn't they think of us as ideal prospective parents? It took less than twenty-four hours to have that belief well and truly shattered; at over thirty-five, Peter was too old.

In no uncertain terms, I was informed that the majority of mothers considering giving their babies up for adoption were in their late teens. These young girls had already decided that their parents, who themselves were usually only in their late thirties or early forties, were too old to care for the child. Why, therefore, would they want strangers of that age to have custody? Why, indeed? So I did keep trying to get pregnant, and I was lucky. But it made me realize that unless we find ourselves in the situation where the possibility of becoming pregnant naturally does not exist, we cannot possibly hope to comprehend why some couples choose alternative routes to parenthood. For some people, facing a life without children is simply not an option, and they have chosen a different, but equally fulfilling, path to parenthood.

Through the wonders of modern medicine, many couples

today are offered the kind of hope that their parents' generation could have only dreamt about. Wanting to have a child but facing childlessness has always been viewed as unacceptable, and the advances in methods of intervention enabling parenthood bear witness to this.

From the moment we witnessed the birth of Louise Brown, the world's first test-tube baby, we have seen medical science move on in leaps and bounds; today, not only do we have in vitro fertilization, we also have available a multitude of other assisted reproductive techniques.

Adoption and surrogacy are still always worth considering, and although neither is as available as some may wish, when they can be achieved, they offer a fulfillment that might otherwise never have been possible. Surrogacy is still a relatively new concept, and there have been only a few cases of it—and still fewer people who are prepared to talk about their experience. Therefore only a single example could be included in this chapter, and it makes a valuable contribution to our understanding of the strength and determination some couples find when faced with life without children.

DONNA'S STORY

IT HAS been several years since we lost our beautiful twins, Emma and Tom. Sometimes I feel like it all happened so long ago, and other times I feel as though it was yesterday, because every detail of what happened is still so vivid in my mind.

My husband, David, and I had wanted a child for many, many years. We received various forms of treatment without success, until eventually we decided that going on the gamete intrafallopian transfer (GIFT) program was the only option left. To our absolute surprise and happiness, I became pregnant on the first attempt, and we soon discovered that I was having twins. We were so delighted that even a small problem that arose at eight weeks didn't mar our excitement.

When I reached the twenty-week stage, I decided it was safe enough to start buying a few things for the babies, and I can still remember how excited I was to actually have some baby things in the house. Even feeling the babies move was so incredible. I used to spend ages looking in the mirror at my expanding stomach, because I was so big and I loved it. We felt so sure that everything was going to be okay. Although I knew of other people who had lost their babies late in their pregnancies, including my sister, we were sure it wasn't going to happen to us after we'd waited so long.

One night, when we'd been out for dinner with some friends, we arrived home quite early, and I was feeling fine. Then I had the strangest feeling, and my waters broke. I remember so clearly the feeling of dread as I kept thinking this could not be happening to me. I went straight to the hospital, where I lay for nearly a week, praying that somehow everything would be all right. Deep down, though, we knew things were wrong, and late one night I went into labor. It lasted for about five hours and then it stopped, leaving us hanging on to that last shred of hope. It started again the next night. This time it stopped after three hours, putting us on an emotional roller-coaster ride, expecting the worst but praying for a miracle.

Sadly, although the labor had stopped, our little girl had decided that it was time to come into the world. Her head was engaged, ready to be born, and there was no fluid left in her sac. There was no choice but to put me under an anesthetic and deliver her. My wonderful doctor explained everything to us, and we thought this was the end. Imagine our confusion when we discovered that we had lost our little girl but that our other baby had decided to stay with us. I had lost a baby, but I was still pregnant.

The midwife who had sat with me all night was so kind and gentle. She told us how beautiful our baby was and asked if I would like to see her. I couldn't bear it at first, but the nurse showed me some photographs and I could see she was beautiful— so perfect, but just too tiny to survive. When I was ready, they wheeled her cradle into my room, and I felt I was going to break in two. I watched as Jenny bathed her, and then she wrapped her gently and gave her to me. This was my baby. I was a mom. If only she would cry. Couldn't this be a mistake? Could she just be sleeping? We wanted these precious babies more than anything in the world. I cried until I was so exhausted there was nothing left. I was devastated at losing our darling little girl, but trying to keep some strength for the baby still inside me.

As I was unable to leave the hospital, we had a funeral service for Emma there, and I watched our beautiful daughter in a little white coffin covered in pink roses. The service was lovely, but all I could think was, Please let me take her home. I just wanted to take her home with me. For the next two weeks, I lay in that hospital bed holding my stomach and begging my other baby to stay there. I was nearly twenty-six weeks pregnant, so close to the time when, if the baby were born, he would have a better chance of survival. Then suddenly labor started again, and I couldn't believe it. I wanted to be able to go to sleep for a couple of weeks and then wake up to find everything was fine, but it wasn't to be.

A scan showed him kicking and moving, with his little heart still beating well, but after a three-hour labor our beautiful son Tom was born. I held him in my arms and cuddled him. For so many years I had imagined being in this room and hearing my baby cry, but now there was nothing. We had buried our little girl, and now our little boy lay lifeless in my arms.

After four long, long weeks in the hospital, Dave and I drove home alone, and I really don't know how I went on living. When Dave left for work in the mornings, I would stay in bed thinking that maybe, if I stayed there long enough, I'd die. It was what I wanted. I remember the first time we drove to the cemetery to see where Emma and Tom were buried—I believed that if another car hit us and killed us both, it would be for the best. I couldn't leave Dave on his own, but I didn't want to live anymore, and I couldn't understand how everyone around us was able to go on with their lives when my babies were dead.

Seven months later, I became pregnant again naturally. It was a long pregnancy, fraught with worry and fear, but today we have a beautiful little girl named Rhiannon. She is our miracle, and nothing could ever describe the feelings of joy when we first heard her cry.

I survived with the love of my husband and my family. A friend of mine sent me a card on which these words of Abraham Lincoln were written: "You can not now realize that you will ever feel better—and yet you are sure to be happy again."

SANDRA'S STORY

I HAVE found that having infertility problems and enduring miscarriages has caused me a great amount of grief and misery. It has been a long, hard road, although perhaps not as long as some may have to endure.

My first two pregnancies were with the assistance of an oral fertility drug called Clomid. Its purpose is to help ovulation occur, and it was here that my problem lay. Fourteen months after we first tried to start a family, we finally found I was pregnant, and I felt great. There was no morning sickness, I continued to walk and swim and to maintain my fitness and health. My first checkup confirmed the pregnancy and found that all was well, so I thought everything was going to be a breeze.

At twelve weeks, I went in for another checkup to monitor the baby's heartbeat and check on my progress generally. I was still feeling very confident, so I couldn't believe it when the doctor started telling me that there seemed to be a problem, because he couldn't find the heartbeat. A scan later that day confirmed that my baby had in fact died between six and eight weeks. I couldn't believe that for so many weeks I had been carrying around my dead baby, because it hadn't expelled itself. I never knew a miscarriage could happen like that, and throughout the twenty-minute journey home, I could hardly see anything as the tears streamed down my face.

Although the whole episode was extremely traumatic, I was optimistic that, as I'd managed to get pregnant once, I could do it again. But two weeks after my dilation and curettage I was still bleeding, and investigations showed some tissue had been left behind. I had to have another dilation and curettage, and knowing that made all the grief and recriminations return. I endured that operation, and then, two weeks later, I was laid off. My self-esteem was at an all-time low; I couldn't keep a baby or a job—I was a failure, and the self-pity was consuming me.

Soon afterwards, though, I found a new job, and later that year my husband and I went to Europe for a long holiday. When we returned, I started taking Clomid again, and eight months after the miscarriage, I was pregnant again.

This time I did have morning sickness, and it stayed throughout the first twelve weeks. My mother assured me it was a good sign, but I was still constantly filled with panic and anxiety. Paul came with me for the scan, but because of the sickness, we actually felt quite confident that things were fine. I thought I was going to go mad when the nurse who was doing the scan called in a doctor and he told me the same thing had happened again. My baby had died weeks before, but the sickness had remained because the placenta had continued to grow.

It took seven months for my periods to return, and even then it was only with the help of progesterone and estrogen. The doctors believed that the three dilation and curettages had left the lining of my uterus too thin, so I was referred to a specialist. They also believed that the Clomid had run its course and was therefore no longer effective, but we had one more unsuccessful attempt.

At the in vitro fertilization clinic, I began a program of ovulation induction that involved daily hormone injections to encourage the production of eggs in my ovaries. They explained that this production and my hormone levels would then be monitored by blood tests and an ultrasound every second day. If and when I then produced two or three good-sized eggs, they would induce ovulation via another hormone injection and then tell us what time to have intercourse. First, though, they had to get my periods to return, and this was to be where my luck swung.

The day before my in vitro fertilization appointment, my periods returned naturally. The next day, I began the program, feeling healthy, fit, and full of confidence. After a few shaky attempts, my husband got the hang of the injections. He was so supportive and I reacted so well to the hormones that I produced nine eggs that were suitable to be fertilized.

We then had to change tacks and begin treatment at the clinic. My husband had to give a sperm sample while they removed the majority of the eggs from my ovaries, leaving behind just a few, which they attempted to fertilize by artificial insemination. We were sent home, and a week later, following a few more hormone injections, it was confirmed that I was pregnant again. The treatment had produced a better-quality egg, and the chances, they said, of having another miscarriage were slim.

In July 1991, I gave birth to my darling daughter, Monique. It was the best day of my life! Over the past few years, many people have asked why I don't tell them I'm pregnant until I'm "safe." It's strange, but if that were the case, maybe I should tell them only after a baby is born. But what I know is that these are my family and friends, and they care. These are the people who are there to support me when things don't go according to plan, the ones I have shared my sorrow and my grief with, and the ones who helped me continue in the belief that one day I'd have a child.

I also have a strong, loving partner who has been my savior. I always knew that even if we didn't have any children, then we at least would always have each other.

TRACEY'S STORY

OVER AN eight-year period, I had ten pregnancies. Starting in 1989, I went on to have three miscarriages, chromosomal tests, pelvis X rays, blood tests, and then an ectopic pregnancy. They discovered our problem was immunological, so in an effort to counteract the problem, they transferred some of my husband's blood into me, hoping to build up antibodies. I still didn't become pregnant, and a later laparoscopy showed adhesions in my tubes from the ectopic pregnancy.

Finally, we commenced the in vitro fertilization program and undertook the preliminary tests. During the course of these tests, I became pregnant, and in early 1993, as a result of the antibody treatment, I gave birth to a healthy baby girl. Throughout the pregnancy, I had been panic-stricken in case something went wrong; even when they performed an emergency cesarean, I worried that I would go home empty-handed again. We were lucky, and I've never been so happy or smiled so much. I had finally achieved, and I walked around on pure adrenalin getting on with the job that lay before me—I was a mother now.

In late 1993, I became pregnant again, and even though I knew looking after two babies so close in age was going to be hard, I didn't care. If it didn't rain, it poured, and how fantastic that we were going to have an instant family after all we'd been through. It wasn't to be, as once again I had a miscarriage, but I told myself how lucky I was to have one child, and I spoiled her totally. It was rare for her not to sleep in our bed; I was scared of crib death, but mostly I just wanted her close to us. She went everywhere with us.

As we were going through all the difficulties, we became very different people. We were less sociable, less friendly, and totally guarded in our relationships with others. In hindsight, I wonder whether, had we behaved differently, we might have been more empowered. I pushed my emotions deep within me, and I didn't cry. I began to eat more and did little for my appearance, because I was punishing myself. I became aggressive, which was a sign of my depression and the huge chip I carried around on my shoulder. I'm still trying to chisel that chip away.

One day, our daughter told us she would like a little sister, so after very little thought, we decided to try again. More disappointment—another miscarriage, then another and another. I was convinced I would never have another child, but I remained as desperate for another one as I had been for the first.

As a last resort, we underwent the immunological antibody treatment again. It is not always necessary to have that treatment twice, but the doctor felt that after five years it was probably worth trying. Ten months later, and we had a new baby son. Our lives are now so enriched; the children adore each other, and every night I thank God for giving them to me.

I know that I have started the healing process, and I now consciously work toward being the person I was before. Despite everything, I suppose I've actually changed for the better.

JANE'S STORY

OVER THE past seven years, I have suffered nine early miscarriages. Initially I was told that this was caused by a lack of progesterone during pregnancy, and I was prescribed pessaries. However, it soon became apparent that this was not the direct cause of the problem, as the miscarriages continued. All the tests the doctor carried out failed to come up with a solution.

Eventually, James and I went to see an immunologist, and through a series of blood tests, he discovered that I had a thickening of the blood in the placenta. Although the doctor prescribed aspirin and a mild steroid, and then aspirin and injected heparin, I still went on to have three miscarriages.

The immunologist suggested that I could be a candidate for a transfusion of my husband's white blood cells, so we went ahead, and I was injected with his blood cells in fourteen places over my body. Shortly afterwards, I had another miscarriage.

There seemed to be no answers to my problem. I even started to look for answers of my own, searching books and contacting a clinic in London I'd been told specialized in treating recurring miscarriage. The books gave me answers I'd already considered and dismissed, and the clinic was just too far away, so my frustration grew. We were desperate; my husband was approaching forty and he wanted children as much as I did, and neither of us knew where our lives would lead without them.

In desperation, I started to look around for alternative treatment, and I went to see a Chinese doctor in Sydney's Chinatown. I took a combination of herbs for six months and then had a six-month course of acupuncture, but both were to no avail. I even began to think that what was happening was in my head, that my subconscious was actually willing me to miscarry each pregnancy, so I tried hypnotherapy. By this stage, even my husband thought I was mad, grasping at straws and attempting anything that crossed my path.

My husband and I found ourselves avoiding dinner parties where there were parents of young children; we avoided any situation where we might leave feeling sad. I found I was almost angry when friends or family members became pregnant, thinking, Why not me? I suppose it was knowing this that made my sister-in-law and my closest friend keep their pregnancies from me for as long as they could, but it still upsets me that they did.

Every so often, we would visit a doctor in Canberra to reassess the file and to see if there was a solution we might have missed. One thing that came up now and then in the discussions was surrogacy. Because I could get pregnant easily but miscarried each pregnancy at an early stage, the doctor was convinced that the problem lay with my immune system and a natural rejection of the pregnancy. He believed that surrogacy might be an option. Someone else could carry the baby for me, and that child would be our own biologically.

From the beginning, I didn't have any problem with the concept of surrogacy, but my husband couldn't understand why someone else would want to carry a baby for us. Nevertheless, as I have no sisters or close female relative, nor does my husband, I started to make inquiries, and initially I found only a few unsuitable candidates. One woman wanted to go to the newspapers and sensationalize the story for profit; another was divorced but still wanted another child. With them both I saw red lights.

Then I found Kate, a divorced mother of three who had had her tubes tied and definitely didn't want any more children of her own. She had a burning desire to be a surrogate mother for purely altruistic reasons, and she was just wonderful. We started the long process of seeing counselors, doctors, and lawyers. There are many, many legal ramifications surrounding surrogacy, and we were determined that we should progress within the framework that exists; the problems that many of us hear about undoubtedly arise where the guidelines are not adhered to. We had reports prepared, and our case was presented to an ethics committee, and at the end of it all, our case was approved.

Today, James and I are the proud parents of a baby boy and girl. Kate is the most amazing, kindhearted person, who simply wanted to help a couple like us. With all she went through during the pregnancy and the birth, I remained in awe of the fact that what she did, she did for us. It takes a very special person to be prepared to commit herself to such a selfless act, and Kate is that very special person.

Throughout all of the sad experiences we had, I found myself on an emotional roller coaster, going from happy and optimistic to angry and sorry for myself. I tried to talk myself out of any kind of depression by telling myself there's always someone who's worse off than I am. I actually counted myself lucky for being able to get pregnant in the first place, because I knew of people who hadn't even managed that, and gradually I took on a "what will be, will be" approach to life.

I survived with a close network of friends who endured many of my problems and a lot of tears with me over the years. I believe that out of adversity some of us can find strength and determination, and even though at the time it doesn't seem so, we can benefit from our difficult experiences.

However rare the opportunities for assisted reproductive techniques and surrogacy are, and however controversial they may appear, they do remain possibilities to be considered. The tragedy, of course, is that even these special babies may not survive to realize their own miracle of life. Nevertheless, to those men and women who through research and development have given these opportunities to so many, we say thank you.

My greatest sympathy, in compiling this book, lies with those whose stories have no happy ending. But life, as many of us know, does not always offer a happy ending. While most women who suffer the death of a child do go on to have successful pregnancies and go on, therefore, to enjoy the gift of motherhood, there remain thousands who are denied that privilege.

LOUISE'S STORY

MY HUSBAND and I started trying for a baby in 1994. After years without success, we sought the advice of a specialist and discovered that my husband's sperm count was low. There followed several attempts by various methods for me to become pregnant: artificial insemination, in vitro fertilization with a microinjection, and finally pronuclear staged transfer (PROST). In the process, they took twenty-three eggs from me, but unfortunately the eggs were immature, and only three fertilized to become embryos. I had been hyperstimulated for these eggs, so they decided to freeze the embryos. We were terrified that they would not survive the freezing and then the thawing, but luckily they did, and the three embryos were transferred via pronuclear staged transfer. We could do nothing more but wait, and eventually, two days after my period had been due, a blood test confirmed that I was pregnant at last. My husband and I just stood there and cried.

I didn't let myself get too excited about the baby or believe that everything was okay until I reached the eighteen-week mark. As Christmas approached, I was nineteen weeks pregnant, so when I received a gift of some money, I went out and for the first time bought myself some maternity clothes. My excitement and confidence were growing with each passing week, and I couldn't wait.

My baby had started to move at fifteen weeks, but from Boxing Day onwards, I became aware that the movement had stopped. I just knew that something was wrong. People told me not to worry, that it was early to feel the baby move anyway, but whatever they said to me, I knew they were wrong. Finally I went to see the doctor, and although he tried very hard, he couldn't find the heartbeat, and the scan that followed couldn't detect any movement. I was in absolute shock, and all I could do was rock backwards and forwards while a nurse asked me if I would like a cup of tea. I wanted to die, not drink tea.

I was taken to the labor ward, where I could hear the cries of newborn babies all around me. I wanted to get the baby out, but as they began to induce labor, the worst experience of my life followed. Labor is terrible at the best of times, but in most cases there is a beautiful baby to hold afterwards and the pain is soon forgotten. For me there was pain and then nothing.

I delivered a tiny son, and in some ways we were lucky; we spent about half an hour holding him. We counted his fingers and toes and even realized that he had his father's flat feet. We have two special photos of Jack, and we have his foot- and hand-prints and a tiny little armband, but when we left the hospital the next day, I still felt that I had left something behind.

We had a cremation service for Jack with only my husband and I there, and this gave us a sense of completion. On the day he was due to be born, we scattered his ashes in a special place we both love. Spending that time with him was important; he looked so perfect, and we now have those memories of our boy. Today, we are saving up to have another try. We are both terri-fied, but what option do we have? Having a family is all I have ever wanted.

RHONDA'S STORY

IF SOMEONE had told me on my wedding day in December 1972, that my husband and I wouldn't have children, I might have said, "That's all right, I'm marrying for love, not to have children." With hindsight, it would have been a most ignorant remark, but I was young and not ready to have children at that point.

We were working on a seven-year plan before starting our fam-ily, and eventually, in 1979, we decided the time had come. We were full of expectation, although, knowing that some of our friends had had problems, I told my husband that if it didn't work out for us I would accept that. I later realized that these were hol-low words, and many times I have regretted what I said.

After two and a half years without success, I began to grow fearful. The tests we had undergone determined that there was a problem; it lay with my husband, and we were told that we would probably never have children. It was devastating news for us both, and we grieved for the child that we knew we would not have. At times like that, however, you do a great deal of soul searching, and for us the soul searching resulted in our decision to commence the Artificial Insemination by Donor Program. It took nine months of waiting, testing, and psychological counseling, but eventually I started attending the clinic. To everyone's amazement, I became pregnant after the second month of treatment; I was told I was very fertile.

This was a very special baby for us both, as it had taken three and a half years to make. I felt the weight of the world lift off my shoulders, and we felt that all the physical and emotional pain, all the tears and the hurt, were behind us. Then, when I was into my thirteenth week, I started to hemorrhage. I called the specialist, who told me to go to bed and rest. I called him every day, but he refused to see me, believing that all was well with the baby. After two weeks, I finally decided to arrange an ultrasound for myself, and as I lay there they told me my baby was dead.

I went into the hospital the next day to have the baby "removed." I was inconsolable; I didn't want to see or talk to anyone, and I can't describe the pain of being in a maternity ward with empty arms. With the depression that set in afterwards, I sought medical help. I needed understanding, but after three visits it wasn't forthcoming, so I simply stopped going.

The most heartbreaking part for me was that all our family and friends were now either pregnant or already had children. While we were trying to have one baby, my husband's sister had had three, and she didn't seem to understand our pain. She asked us to be godparents to her new baby, and when I explained it was just too soon for me, communication broke down and disharmony set in with the family.

For me time stood still. I had to wait three months before I could begin treatment again, and when I did, they found that my hormone levels had dropped dramatically; I never ovulated at the same level again. As the months turned into years, I became more withdrawn. I was put on fertility drugs, but nothing ever happened. I felt a failure. I felt depressed and guilty, and I had changed from a happy person into a very withdrawn and unhappy one.

As the years passed by, the desire for a child grew deeper and deeper. My husband said that if we couldn't have children, then I was all he wanted, but sadly that wasn't enough for me—I felt like an empty shell. I wanted to be pregnant so much that in desperation I even slept with someone outside the marriage. I didn't think I had anything to lose, and I thought my marriage was rock solid. I was forgetting, after all the clinical processes we'd been subjected to in the past, that I still had feelings. I didn't get pregnant, and finally, after eight years of being totally miserable, depressed, and confused, I ended my marriage.

For a while I lived in rent-shared accommodations, and then, in 1988, injuries from a car accident ten years earlier seemed to reemerge and intensify. I was in chronic pain, severely depressed, unable to earn a living, unable to have children, guilt-ridden because of my broken marriage, and trying to live with shattered dreams.

Feeling that I had nothing to live for, I tried to take my own life in January 1990. Obviously I wasn't successful, but I realize now that this was a turning point in my life. I found a caring and understanding psychiatrist, and I was well cared for by other hospital staff and my close friends. My brother and his family also embraced me with love, and gradually, with the help of support groups and others, my life improved. I accepted that I would probably be on my own for the rest of my life, accepted that I would never have children. Then, out of the blue, I met a wonderful, caring man in 1991, and in November of 1992 we married.

Sometimes I look back on my past and, deep down, I will always regret that I could not have a child, but I accept it now, because I did all that was possible to have my own baby. I didn't cope very well, but this is my life, and I handled it the only way I could. Best of all is that I have forgiven myself finally and let go of the guilt.

Cheryl's Story

In March 1998, my husband dragged me to the doctor because, at forty-one years of age, I was feeling bone-weary, bloated, and nauseous. Much to our amusement, the doctor ran a pregnancy test, more to rule out possibilities than in the belief that I was actually pregnant. We had been trying half-heartedly to have children for years, but we had reached the point where we realized it wasn't going to happen for us and had started to make other plans for our lives.

Imagine, then, the feelings that coursed through us when the doctor calmly announced, "Well, that's positive." I was suddenly soaring and can still relive the elation I felt. It was like I'd been chosen and had entered some other world. So began our odyssey of the highest of highs mixed with earth-shattering lows.

On the day we went in for a scan, the sight of that tiny heartbeat reinforced the miracle of life. As I lay there happily, the technician saw another shadow on the screen and explained to us that she'd have to explore further. Suddenly, these two childless people were expecting twins! My world crashed, and I couldn't stop crying. I felt as if God was playing a huge joke on us as; at times I thought it was all going to be fine and at others I wondered how on earth we'd ever cope. As visions of all the special-needs children I'd ever taught came back, we seesawed from feelings of excitement and joy to feelings of sheer terror. Our general practitioner was very calm and matter-of-fact; it seemed like no one really understood how we were feeling. For our own peace of mind, we decided to see a specialist and find out more about amniocentesis and other tests.

At the time, we decided not to tell our families about the pregnancy. They were all out of the area, and it was hard enough coping with our own feelings without being worried for them as well. During the two weeks we waited to see the specialist, we talked endlessly as we never had before. We cried, agonized, and became excited all at the same time, and we began to dream and plan for our little babies' lives.

As soon as the specialist began to scan my belly looking for the heartbeats, I knew. I looked at the two little bundles that had previously been rhythmically beating and I knew. As he confirmed that there were no longer any heartbeats, the darkness closed in on me; I thought it was my fault. I'd been too worried, I'd panicked. How on earth could these two little innocents survive when I'd been so bad? Although the doctor tried to reassure me that none of these fears were true, I didn't believe him.

He talked to us about the need for a curettage but part of me rebelled against the outside world dragging my babies away. Another part of me wanted the operation, but as it was a Saturday, we would have to wait until Monday anyway before anything could be done. I have never experienced anything like those gut-wrenching sobs that came from deep within me that day.

Somehow we got through it all. We did tell our families, and they supported us and cried with us. It seemed that I heard it all and saw it all from a great distance, becoming increasingly aware of the platitudes and how easily they rolled off people's tongues. I questioned my past support of parents in distressing situations and realized I had been just as inadequate. To make it worse, my husband hated to see me cry, so I tried to keep my feelings to myself. He didn't want to talk, and I wanted to keep talking, but there was no one to talk to; no one seemed to understand. I realized that no one even mentioned it; it was as if I was expected to simply move on with my life as if nothing had happened. In my confusion, I started to question whether or not it had happened at all and whether I was even sane. I so wanted to talk to others, but if I tried, the tears and sobbing began.

Finally, I got frightened by my own lethargy and depression, so I sought help. I phoned a grief counselor, and I read what I could find on the subject, and I learned that what I was going through was normal. I read that other women who had suffered miscarriages took refuge in chocolate or hugged their teddy bears to death, and I discovered that the brick wall developing between my husband and me was due to our different ways of grieving, nothing more.

Nevertheless, I felt so lonely and desolate. I wrote letters to my babies and stayed in bed crying and looking at their ultrasounds. As a teacher, my life had revolved around the power of words, but suddenly there were no words and no way to describe what I felt. These were our children we had lost; I saw myself reading bedtime stories, teaching them to swim and to love the birds and animals around us, and I saw them jumping on our bed, laughing, full of life—and on and on. I had never realized I'd even wanted children, and now, at forty-one years old, it was too late.

My babies are always there, and I carry that experience with me forever. However, I can laugh again now, and I appreciate the small glimpses of beauty in this life, things I would probably have never seen otherwise.

ANNIE'S STORY

A LOT of times, when I'm feeling sad, I call my husband, and then I feel a little better. Philip and I met at work. He had been asking me out for a year before I accepted, but the first time we went out, we knew we were going to marry and spend forever together. When we married, we bought a house that needed some work done to it, so we set about doing it in preparation for Jessica Rose or Dominic Alexander.

After six months without success, I began to worry about my chances of getting pregnant. Philip was more positive than I was, but still I felt we ought to seek some help. We eventually saw a few specialists, and they found that Philip's sperm count was low, meaning it would be necessary for him to have a varicocelectomy operation. Following the operation, we had to wait six months before trying to get me pregnant, but then, in March 1997, we finally found out I was pregnant. I didn't believe it; at last our lives were going to be complete—or so we thought. During my first ultrasound, they found that I had fibroids, but not knowing what they were, I wasn't particularly worried. As it turned out, though, my gynecologist explained that my condition was actually likely to get out of hand and result in difficulties. I became so sick that I was in and out of the hospital constantly, and the nausea stayed with me for twenty-four hours a day, seven days a week.

The fibroids became bigger, and I had to take medication to stop the poison from reaching the placenta, where it would harm the baby. Everything was wasted, though, when the medication didn't work and Jessica was stillborn at twenty-four weeks. That day in July 1997 was the darkest day of our lives, and we both still cry a lot for what we have lost, thinking of how it could have been.

Six months later, I had the fibroids removed, all fourteen of them, but six weeks after that, my doctor found that two more fibroids had grown. We were sick and tired of disappointments, and to make matters worse, these two were inside my uterus, whereas the others had been outside. They could not be removed, but the doctor told us I should still be able to get pregnant. He was wrong, so a few months later we started on a program called intrauterine insemination (IUI) at the in vivo fertilization clinic. By this stage, Philip's sperm count was normal; my ovaries, tubes, and uterus were fine; and my periods were back to normal. Things were looking quite good, and on the second attempt I found myself pregnant again. Eight weeks later, I had a miscarriage and we were devastated.

Philip and I have now tried intrauterine insemination five times without any further success. We will go on and have one more try, but if that doesn't work we may have to try in vitro fertilization. We don't really want to do that; it's expensive and we don't have a lot of money, but what can you do? You have to try everything, and you have to have hope and faith. The memories remain so clear in my mind, and Philip and I still talk often about the children we'll never have. Philip devotes his life to me and to our having a baby together. He has been my light every day, and I hope I have been his.

CHERRELL'S STORY

MY FIRST pregnancy was at twenty-three and ended in a miscarriage. The relationship I was in ended soon afterwards, and I spent the next few years getting a business degree and concentrating on building a satisfying career. I met my husband when I was thirty-five; we married the following year and tried for a family straightaway, but the first pregnancy ended at seven weeks. This was to be the start of my nightmare, which hasn't ended. There is only one thing that looks certain now, and that is that I will never be a mother.

After six months of trying to get pregnant again, without success, I was referred to a gynecologist who worked within one of Queensland's leading in vitro fertilization groups. He did some exploratory surgery and found that my fallopian tubes were blocked at the entrance to the uterus and that there was extensive damage to other areas. He also found that I had only one tube, although I did have both ovaries. All told, it meant that my only hope was in vitro fertilization, and the fact that I'd been pregnant quite recently made me a good candidate.

I found this news extremely hard to accept. How could so much damage have been done in only six months, with no infections or anything else out of the ordinary? It just didn't make any sense to me, but as I liked and trusted this doctor, I started on the in vitro fertilization program. I was in a hurry because of my age; a lot of women don't realize that our fertility rate drops quickly after the age of thirty-five. If you run into problems, as I did, then you haven't left yourself much time for error. Over the next two years, I underwent in vitro fertilization treatment every three months, without success. On each occasion the treatment involved twenty needles in my arm, ten to fifteen bigger needles in my bottom (these hurt like hell), an operation, and then two weeks of waiting and praying to God that this time there would be a pregnancy. It was almost like having to live at the doctor's office because of the amount of monitoring that was necessary. However, I still held down my job and spent all of my disposable income on medical gap bills.

Two years and eight unsuccessful treatments later, my doctor still told me there was no reason why I hadn't gotten pregnant—except, of course, my age and the impact this has on the quality of my embryos. I had considered the option of microsurgery to fix my fallopian tube, but was discouraged from pursuing this course of action due to the limited chances of its success. Our options were few, so ultimately my husband and I decided to apply to adopt a child from overseas. I was now thirty-eight years old and my husband had just turned forty-seven. I'd spent some time living in Asia as a child, and I loved the idea of an Asian child, but the cruelest blow was yet to come. We were told that our application had been turned down; we were not eligible to adopt a child from overseas, as my husband was six months over the state's maximum age limit for adoptive parents. At thirty-eight, I had just been sentenced to a life of childlessness because of six lousy months. The legislation governing this decision is so strong that even the antidiscrimination department couldn't help me.

I couldn't and wouldn't give up. My endeavors and constant failures to become a mother were starting to take their toll on me, but I couldn't face life without a child. In desperation I booked to have the operation on my tube, despite the earlier warnings that it was unlikely to succeed. When I awoke from the surgery, I was given the best news yet; I didn't need major surgery after all, my Fallopian tube was perfectly normal, just blocked at the entrance to the uterus from a part of the miscarriage that hadn't cleared.

Twenty minutes and $200 had fixed the one thing that had stopped my getting pregnant over all those years. I hadn't needed to have the in vitro fertilization treatments—with all the pain, anguish, and expense they'd involved—at all. Now I was three years older, and I'd lost three vital years of my remaining fertility. Becoming pregnant would be harder now than ever, and no one knew what impact the enormous amount of drugs I'd taken might have on the quality of my eggs.

One year after that operation, I'm still not pregnant and, at forty years of age, it looks like it may never happen. What has happened has taken a huge toll on my life. I don't know if anyone can help fix a broken heart caused by childlessness, but I've sought help anyway. I thought I was in danger of slipping into a deep depression, but the diagnosis is not depression, just grief.

Nowhere to Lay the Flowers

Nothing can relieve the pain
When an unborn child is lost
Only a mother's hopes and dreams
Mourned, and she counts the cost
There will be no plaque, "In Memory"
Nowhere to lay the flowers
Just an emptiness inside her,
To fill with grieving hours.
Those of us who've suffered
Know the pain and share the load
We are right there beside you,
For we've trodden your lonely road
Nothing will erase the grieving,
Only time will ease the pain
Gather strength from those who love you
And be prepared to live again.

(BY COLLEEN, IN MEMORY OF HER BABY)

Through the Years

TIME, THEY SAY, IS A GREAT HEALER. TIME IS IN FACT
not a healer at all. It is merely a period in our lifetime during which we learn to come to terms with
whatever tragedy has befallen us. It is a period of facilitation for
the grieving process we must all endure.

As hard as it still is today to openly grieve over a miscarriage
without feelings of shame or guilt, most of us can only imagine
what it was like for women in the past. Thirty or forty years ago,
sex and childbirth were most certainly not topics for open dis-
cussion. It is understandable, therefore, that discussing the death

of a baby was considered almost abhorrent in any social circle. Some of the letters I received from women told of how they had not known about their mothers' miscarriages until they themselves had one. Only at that point did their mothers, in an effort to comfort and support them, talk about their loss—and in doing so finally feel they were able to grieve more openly and honestly than ever before.

The situation was sometimes made worse by a male culture still firmly entrenched in chauvinism: this was a generation of men raised to leave women's business to the women, to express no emotion, and to continue on regardless. Hence many of the women who experienced this loss were given no choice but to grieve in silence and to grieve alone. But those men must have suffered just as much as men today do, and I wonder at the long-term impact caused by the suppression of their emotions.

I was truly saddened when I read my own parents' accounts of the day my elder sister's twin died. I knew that Carolyn had had a twin, but the ramifications of her death and the long-term effect that it had on my parents was not something we had really discussed before. It struck me for the first time how neither of my parents had healed after that experience; they, like many of their generation, had simply moved on.

It was with enormous gratitude that I realized how a great many women of that generation saw the research for this book as an opportunity to finally speak out and, as they said, to begin a more open grieving process, this time without shame. In the following stories you will read the experiences of women whose babies died many, many years ago. They each got through that painful time and have continued with their lives, but through the years, while the pain and the grief might have eased, the sadness and sense of great loss remain.

HAZEL'S STORY

ROBERT WAS born in 1963 and lived for three days. The whole scenario involved many mistakes. At the time we were living where there was only a small local hospital and a few local general practitioners. I wasn't seeing a specialist, just my own general practitioner, who had delivered two of my other three children without any problems and whom, therefore, I trusted to deliver my fourth baby. There was never any reason to think otherwise, and anyway, in those days women just had babies—it wasn't considered a big thing. Today there's much more specialization and more understanding and a much more general body of knowledge amongst people.

In the weeks leading up to Robert's birth, I started to feel that something wasn't quite right. I said to my general practitioner, "It feels wrong, it feels wrong, it doesn't feel...comfortable." By your fourth pregnancy, you have an understanding of how your body changes and what the emotional and physical responses are to those changes. As it turned out, I had placenta previa, and—as even happens today without adequate diagnosis and treatment— the cards were stacked against the chances of a successful delivery.

My memories of the event are surrounded by feelings of cold, miserable, and depressing conditions. The whole thing was just awful. I was left, for what seemed like a lifetime, lying on a gurney in the hospital passageway. I was alone, it was the middle of the night, and I think there were no surgeons on duty at the time. The baby was heaving, and I remember pressing the bell and calling out, "This baby's trying to get born!" I really didn't know what was going on around me, and I didn't ask questions, because I wasn't feeling up to it.

At some stage it must have become clear to the doctors and nurses that I would need to have an emergency cesarean section, but apparently, before they could operate, I needed a blood transfusion. Bob and one of our neighbors had to jump into the car and drive like maniacs to the city to get blood and bring it back to us.

When eventually Robert was born, he was in trouble; the placenta was born first, so he was starved of oxygen. As I understand it, the surgery was not done soon enough, and all the while his oxygen supply was being restricted. Apparently, though, he looked fine, and Bob, who saw him straightaway, was so excited. Unfortunately, I never got to see or hold him at all, because the facilities at the hospital were quite poor and Robert needed to be put in an incubator. They whisked him off to a city hospital, and I was left where I was—left alone with my grief and upset, feeling terribly ill, but knowing I had to find the strength to recover and return home to my other three small children.

To compound it all, there was nowhere set aside for mothers who were without their babies. Instead, I was placed in a two-bed room where the other woman was clearly in pain and spent the night moaning. They put me on an IV drip, and even that went wrong, as it had been poorly administered. If all that had happened today, I'd ask questions about what went wrong, but back then, what would it have achieved? The baby was gone.

Like everyone, I suppose, I question things that happened and wonder whether it was something I did or something that happened that led to the problems. I've never, however, felt personal guilt or the sense of failure I know a lot of other women feel. There are a couple of things I think contributed to what happened, but they will remain in confidence forever.

It took me several weeks to get over the surgery especially, and almost immediately we began the election campaign, leaving no time for anything other than politics and the electorate. We went to live in a rented house, which was left to me to organize and set up. It was like living in a bus station, with people forever wandering in and out. I kept house and I was hospitable, but I didn't get involved fully in the campaign trail, because I just wasn't fit enough.

My other children were going to the local primary school at the time, and that created its own difficulties. There was one woman whom I saw every day when I took the children to the crossing, and she was pregnant at the same time I was. She went on to have a healthy baby girl, and I just couldn't stand it. I found it so difficult to see her and chat, so I avoided her and her baby. I suppose I felt angry and jealous, which is not very pleasant to admit, but it's simply how I felt at the time. Even years later, the death of a child affects things that happen in your life. During the Canberra years, we were friendly with a couple whose child had died when four years old. We were at dinner one evening with other couples and someone remarked on how awful it must have been for them. I said nothing about Robert, but I kept thinking, I've lost a baby, too. I knew that for everyone else he hadn't existed and therefore he wasn't acknowledged, but in my opinion it was even worse for me, because I had never even gotten to know him, whereas the other couple had had four years in which to gather memories. I knew that in some ways it was harder for them, but my feelings were quite negative, and saying anything then didn't seem appropriate.

Throughout it all, when I was very troubled and there was no one I could speak to, I would write my feelings down. It was a way of focusing on what had happened and trying to understand, and it was helpful. What I wrote, though, was just between those pages and me; I wouldn't let anyone see it, not a soul, and when I had finished I would burn it all. It was too intimate, too strong, and too private, but it was a useful process for me to go through.

It's also hard for the other children to deal with the loss of someone who would have been a brother for them. My younger daughter was particularly upset and remained conscious of the loss. I think in a family of four—girl, boy, girl—this next little boy represented her new friend, and suddenly he wasn't there for her. She was so thrilled at the prospect of having a little brother.

Thirty years later, when she had two sons of her own, she found a book called *Loss of a Baby*, by Margaret Nicol, and she said to me, "I'll buy it for you, Mum." We were in Canberra at the time, and the shops there didn't stock the book, so when I went to Sydney, I bought it myself. I couldn't wait to read it, and when I did I just cried and cried. It was a belated release of all the pain for me, because it basically acknowledged everything that happens and how difficult it is to deal with. The book gave legitimacy to the grief and hurt and loss.

I believe those feelings never really go away, and I know I've suppressed a great deal. There are still times when people ask how many children I have, and I want to say four, not three. Without going into long explanations, it's difficult to say you've lost a little boy. There's always, therefore, a sense of incompletion. It's like denying a life, even though that life was a very short one.

As I was so ill after Robert was born, I have little recollection of what happened. He was cremated and his ashes are somewhere in Melbourne, but I've never tried to find out where. Recently, however, it's been different, partly because I've entered a new phase in my life and I'm getting older. There comes a time when it's necessary to attend to unfinished business.

Just recently, Rosslyn said to me, "Mum, one day we'll go down to Melbourne and we'll find Robert's place."

Yes, we will!

Rose's Story

WHEN I was ten weeks pregnant, I leapt into the shower feeling on top of the world, but minutes later my whole world crashed around me. My tiny but perfectly formed baby was expelled, along with all my hopes and dreams.

I picked it up and gently placed it in a little painted box my daughter had left on the side of the bath and rang my friend Donna. Within minutes she was comforting me, and we cried and talked as only girlfriends do. Donna was always one for ceremonies, and this was an occasion that needed to be recognized. We prepared a special plot in the garden, overlooking the harbor, and we laid the tiny coffin to rest.

Donna was pregnant herself, with only a few months left to go, but she shared my pain as only a true friend can. After a few prayers and a long silence, we went inside and poured ourselves a glass of wine. As I played the piano, we sang along to songs like "Feelings" and "Bridge Over Troubled Water," followed by "We'll Meet Again" and "That's What Friends Are For." My friend shared my grief, and because of her I was able to accept my loss and move on with my life. Deep down, I knew that this would be the last time I would go through this pain, as I was already in my forties. I would not and could not go through this again, so I put to rest all ideas of another child. I would be happy with my precious daughter and treasure every moment with her.

Sadly, Donna was diagnosed with breast cancer shortly afterwards, and she passed away a few years ago. But friendship is a precious thing, and Donna's memory lives on in the very special and treasured relationship I now enjoy with her beautiful little daughter, Sophie.

KATHLEEN'S STORY

MY HUSBAND and I have been happily married for forty-nine years. We always intended to have four children, but although my first two pregnancies resulted in the birth of our two healthy, beautiful daughters, over the next eight years I had five miscarriages.

The first miscarriage was a great disappointment, but as I was only twenty-three years old, I was considered young and healthy and was therefore told it was "just one of those things." The second miscarriage was a great shock and quite devastating, as I could not believe this was happening to me. It was at this stage that I began to find the platitudes unacceptable—the usual "It's probably better than having a damaged child;" "You are young, there's plenty of time to have another one;" and the worst one, "Well, it is only an embryo and not yet a child." To us, from the moment we knew I was pregnant, we were having a baby; we never thought of the baby as an embryo or a fetus, so these comments hurt us terribly.

The third miscarriage was like the end of the world for me, and it was with a heavy heart that I started to believe we would never have another child. We carried on trying, though, and the next two miscarriages, while not unexpected, were nevertheless as sad as the others. The investigations carried out into why I seemed unable to sustain a pregnancy merely highlighted a hormonal problem. We were never able to have another child of our own.

I was often told, during those eight painful years, how lucky I was to have two beautiful, healthy children, and indeed I did thank God for that blessing. But they were very difficult years, nonetheless, as at no time was I offered counseling, emotional support, or compassion by the medical profession—or anyone else, for that matter. If anything, doctors were cruel and heartless, even going so far as to accuse me of doing something to interfere with my pregnancies. That was the worst and most shocking reaction I encountered during those years.

My husband and I did not share our grief with anyone else, as we believed others considered what we were going through "no big deal." None of them ever indicated they even understood that these losses, for us, were a tragedy. A great many women had miscarriages, but they were simply never discussed.

For many years following this period in my life, I had nightmares, and they were always the same—feelings of being power-less to stop the death of one of my children—and I would always wake up sobbing with grief.

When our youngest daughter was twelve years old, we fostered a six-year-old boy, and to our joy we were eventually able to adopt him. Today we are proud of our son, our daughters, and our wonderful grandchildren.

Our sadness has been that the girls have also each had a miscarriage. In both cases, though, we grieved with them; we felt their anguish as deeply as we had felt our own, and we supported them in their tragic loss. We know of their appreciation of our understanding and our sharing of their grief.

Helen's Story

I MARRIED at thirty and had my first baby fifteen months later, with some difficulty. He was delivered by cesarean section and died just twenty-five days later.

My next two pregnancies were normal, although there was some bleeding during the early stages; today both children are happy parents. I miscarried my next two pregnancies, and then finally, although I had to stay in bed for many weeks, I gave birth to a healthy son. Today we have a six-foot-two son.

The death of my first child was devastating, but healing came through my Christian faith and the unconditional love of my husband. He also grieved deeply. We both felt the need to be together, to be busy together, and not to ignore the situation, so we frequently talked to one another about what had happened.

Just a few months after our son died, I was asked to sit with a new mother during the funeral service for her stillborn child. I felt a compulsion to do this and shall always be so glad that I did. I just sat with her, and knowing that I too had lost a child, she felt free to ask questions and express her thoughts. Together we said the final prayer of the funeral service: "Let Not Thy Children Be Overwhelmed by Sorrow."

Since then, what was once a terrible experience for me has become a wonderful opportunity to help others practically and with understanding. Today, in everyday life, I am a very happy woman with three married children and twelve lively grandchildren.

JILL'S STORY

I BELIEVE that miscarriage is a tragedy that is not grieved for enough. I am now sixty-four years old, and during my childbearing years, women were expected to recover quickly and pick up their life as if nothing significant had happened to them. I have had only one miscarriage, and it was extremely traumatic and certainly a significant time in my life.

With the Pill still a few years away, I had my first daughter in 1958, within a year of our marriage. I then had difficulty conceiving again, but eventually I gave birth to my second daughter, two years and nine months later. By this time the Pill had become available, but just as I decided that I would give it a try, I found I was pregnant again. We were horrified, because money was a real problem; we were paying off our little house and living on one salary, a bank clerk's.

My mother-in-law, who made it quite clear that she didn't think I could manage one child very well, let alone three, wanted me to have an abortion and even said she would pay for it. With her words ringing in my ears, I spent a night thinking and praying, finally coming to the conclusion that I couldn't possibly have an abortion. I told her and my husband what I had decided and went ahead with the pregnancy.

I went to the local general practitioner, who had looked after me during the previous pregnancy, and all seemed to be well. I began to look forward to the birth of my third child, hoping for the baby son I'd always wanted. At five and a half months, the baby was moving quite strongly, but one night I began bleeding heavily.

We didn't have a car, and we couldn't afford ambulance cover, so my husband had to beg a kind neighbor to take this wildly bleeding lady to the hospital. Wadded with many towels and with my legs in the air, I remained determined not to lose this suddenly ardently wanted baby as I arrived at the hospital. I was devastated, therefore, when, after I'd been admitted, several nuns approached me and demanded to know what I had done to myself. They actually believed that I had tried to abort my own baby.

As I had considered the option of abortion earlier in the pregnancy, I found myself becoming increasingly distressed by the questions. Wild, guilty thoughts went through my mind—did the baby think I didn't want it? Was I being punished for even thinking of getting rid of it? On and on the questions went, haunting me at every turn, until finally the doctor arrived. He persuaded me to lower my legs, and the miscarriage began in earnest. It was horribly like a real birth, with the pain and bearing down as I felt the baby arrive.

My baby was quickly whisked away, and nothing more was said about it. Later, when I asked the doctor the sex of my child, he said he hadn't looked and didn't know. He told me that there was probably something very wrong with the baby, like severe kidney malfunction, as this was often the reason for a miscarriage. I remained in the hospital for a few days, and on the last one I had a curettage and was advised to try for another baby immediately.

I took the advice, and eleven months later we had another beautiful baby girl. Seven years after her arrival, we finally had our son, and it's true that having these children did ease the pain of my loss, but I still grieve for what might have been.

CARMEL'S STORY

TODAY I am in my fifties. I no longer grieve for the infant I lost. Instead, I look back at those times as though my experience happened to someone else, as in fact it did—to a young women in her twenties. I feel sorry for her, for her loss, for the horror that surrounded her at that time and the means by which she survived.

Three young children, a troubled marriage, and another baby on the way was not a good scene to be in. But life goes on, and at the site of the home the couple were building, the young woman helped to dig a trench for the plumber to lay pipes in. All expenses had to be kept to a minimum, but this was to prove an expensive saving.

This was perhaps the only baby I had conceived in happiness or pleasure. The morning sickness was causing me some difficulty, as the three children I was raising were only babies themselves at four, two, and less than one year old. Then one day I started to bleed, and my doctor told me to go to bed and rest. I had no one to look after my children, and my husband couldn't take any time off work, so I carried on as I had before.

When I started to hemorrhage, I was rushed to the hospital, where I found myself being examined by a doctor and felt him remove a large mass from my vagina. I asked him what he had done, and he informed me he was just helping things along, as I was going to lose the baby anyway. I had been brought up a Catholic, and all the fears fed into me over the years came to the fore, so I expressed the need to baptize the infant, no matter how premature. The doctor didn't understand what I was asking, but to my relief and never-ending gratitude, the nurse in attendance told me it had already been done.

Later, I was taken to a ward where I lay in a bed as a handsome young doctor scraped the afterbirth from my womb while at the same time flirting with a pretty young nurse. I felt so shamed by what was happening, and I wanted to shout out, "I'm a woman, I'm here." God, how I could have died at that moment.

The next morning they took me to the operating theater for a curettage. Apparently I had not "lost enough," but in fact they couldn't know what I'd lost, because they simply didn't understand. I was frightened and crying as they wheeled me off, but to them I was just a bothersome patient. When I had recovered from the anesthetic, they pointed me in the general direction of the bathroom, and somehow I got it wrong. I wandered into the wrong room. There were carts in that room and on the carts were bottles and in the bottles were babies. These were the products of spontaneous abortions, and each bore the names of the poor mothers who had lost them.

I was never allowed to grieve for my lost baby. I was expected to just go on with my life as if nothing had happened, and it was only months later, on Mother's Day, that I finally shed a few tears. My dear children gave me some awful red and gold slippers and some burnt toast. How I wished then that my baby could have lived to spend at least a year or two in the love that surrounds little children.

I suffered great shame for my grief, and I believed it to be inappropriate for years, until I received a gift from God. I read a wonderful article about grief and miscarriage that told me it was natural to feel the way I did and natural to cry. Suddenly my grief was comfortable, and finally I could let it go.

MOIRA'S STORY

I LOST a baby boy in 1958—many, many years ago, but one never forgets. My memories of the miscarriage I was not allowed to talk about are still very vivid ones of fright and pain.

I had had a painful night, and in the early hours of the morning I began to bleed heavily. My husband called an ambulance, but I knew as we made our way to the hospital that I'd already lost the baby. Although they kept me in for a few days, no one spoke to me about what had happened; the expectation was clearly that I should just get on with my life and not dwell on this terrible experience. I lay in the ward, teary and in shock, alone in my grief.

Many years later, we were at a family function when I heard my husband telling his sister how precious our firstborn healthy baby was after the loss of this babe. It was only then that I realized how he had grieved as well, but at the time I never knew. Fathers, I now know, also need support when there is a miscarriage, because it is their baby, too.

Today I believe that women can find the support that they so desperately need and that was denied to women in my day. I have learned to accept this experience, and I have been blessed with five healthy children. Each of them was very welcome, and we now have six great-grandchildren. Every May I think of my first babe, sad but accepting.

We all move on and, oh, the absolute feeling of joy we embrace when at last we gaze into the eyes of children we have given birth to. As they return our smile with a hesitant smile of their own we can finally visualize and dream about a future together, forever. But those for whom forever is cut cruelly short must accept the fact that forever is merely as long as the time we are given together. Sometimes we all have to wonder at the level of suffering others have to cope with in their lives and the way in which they find the strength to deal with that suffering and move on. I cannot imagine, after all the babies I have lost, having to then suffer the untimely death of either of my beautiful daughters. Who could? But some of the women in this chapter have had to face this tragedy and have found the strength to share their stories with admirable honesty. The results are extraordinary and offer us a glimpse of strength and humility to which most of us can only aspire.

ANNIE'S STORY

I AM now seventy years old. When I was nineteen years old, I married my childhood sweetheart, who had just completed his medical course, and we moved to the country, where he began work in the local hospital—oh, we were so happy!

Within eighteen months, we had a beautiful baby boy, and although we were keen that he should have a playmate as soon as possible, it wasn't until six years later that I became pregnant again. This time I was pregnant with twins, but when I went into labor five weeks early, our first tragedy struck. The girls weighed seven pounds and three pounds, and sadly the little one, after being cuddled and christened, died. Our one daughter was then examined, and the pediatrician found that she had a heart defect, perhaps a hole in the heart. She was such a beautiful and healthy-looking girl, and she seemed to thrive, but nevertheless we decided to move to another state where we knew there were some excellent heart specialists.

Our daughter continued to thrive under constant observation by the doctors and with the love of all those around her. She looked so well, not even our closest friends knew there was anything wrong with her. When she was twelve years old and moving into her adolescent years, the specialists found she needed an operation, and, thankfully, it went well—her case was written up as a success. After six months, she was fit enough to return to school, and this she did with a renewed vigor for life. She was so happy and full of a new life in which she could take part in all the things she had previously been restricted from doing.

By this stage, I had had another little boy, and my daughter could now enter into the rough and tumble play that was everyday life for the boys. Then suddenly, while she was standing in class and reciting a piece of work, she collapsed and died. We cried and grieved for so long—to think that in her short life she had bravely been through so much. To see her survive such a difficult operation and to lose her now was almost unbearable, and no one, but no one, unless they have been through such an ordeal, could possibly understand.

We grieved together as a family, and with the love, care, and support of one another we became closer then ever before. Four years later, our eldest son, a twenty-two-year-old, six-foot-three champion athlete who never drank or smoked, suddenly died while dancing at a family wedding. It seemed to be the final straw for me, and I was ready to end my own life, but I stopped when I thought, what right have I to put my wonderful husband and darling twelve-year-old son through so much more agony? God obviously meant it to be, so I plodded on with my life. Heaven only knows how—it's harder to continue living than to take the coward's way out and end it all.

Our son grew up to become a doctor, and he chose to specialize in cardiology; today he is successful in his chosen career, and he has children of his own. His father and I were so very proud of him. Five years ago I lost my wonderful soul mate and husband of forty-eight years to a massive coronary. Sadly, I live on until the Almighty calls me to be near my loved ones.

JOY'S STORY

I AM an only child, and as far back as I can remember, I always declared I was going to have a big family. After I married at the age of twenty-one, in 1951, I was told by my gynecologist that I couldn't have children because of previous surgery for two ovarian cysts. Despite it all, though, three years later I was delighted to discover that indeed I could get pregnant, and I went on to have a relatively uneventful pregnancy.

It seemed that my little girl was in no hurry to enter this world until, finally, when I was three weeks overdue, I went into labor. It was a long and difficult labor that ended in the forceps delivery of my eleven-pound daughter. They told me she was stillborn, but I never saw her; they told me it was best if I didn't and assured me that she would be buried in the hospital cemetery. Then they bound my breasts and gave me tablets to stop the milk coming in, but it came anyway. I lay grieving in a room with other mothers who were feeding their newborn babies. I had no one to talk to, no one who could understand what I was going through.

I carried on with my life, seemingly as if nothing had happened, and within the next four years I gave birth to my daughter and my son. In 1961, three years after my son had been born, I became pregnant again, and two weeks before full term, my membranes ruptured and I went into labor. Unfortunately, it was not picked up that I had a shoulder presentation, and what was a most horrifying day ended with an emergency cesarean. The birth was so traumatic that my poor little girl was weakened, and, sadly, she lived only for two days.

As is often the case, my husband and I did not grieve together. We each grieved in our own way, and for my part, I was incapable of letting him into my private world of misery. After thirty-one years of marriage, we finally divorced, and I chose later to go to India and spend time in a Hindu ashram. This provided me with some much needed spiritual and emotional healing that helped me through the next horrific experience in my life when, four years later, my darling son was killed in a senseless road accident just two-thirds of a mile from home.

From all the tragedy I have faced in my life, I have my one daughter. She is now forty-two years old, and she has given me a lovely grandson. I treasure them both so much.

JACKIE'S STORY

WHEN I was twenty-six weeks pregnant with my second child, an ultrasound at our local hospital found that my baby had died. The only clue I had had that something was wrong with the baby was that I hadn't felt any movement for about a week. They told us that, after all the tests they carried out, they couldn't find any heartbeat. We just couldn't believe it; we were so devastated.

To then go through a five-hour labor knowing that at the end of it there would be no baby for us was so hard. When Cody was born, the nurse put him on my tummy; he was so lifeless, it was just tragic. But they placed a bonnet on his head and wrapped him up in a blanket and took some photographs. Those photos are so graphic and so real that every time I look at them I cry.

From that moment, our story has been one of pain, heartbreak, and devastation. Our firstborn son, Luke, who had been diagnosed with cancer, died just months after we lost Cody. So while losing Cody was in itself tragic, we never really had a chance to grieve fully, as we still had a sick little boy to look after, and all of our energy had to be directed toward getting him better. Somehow I feel that perhaps Cody didn't feel the time was right for him to enter the world. I believe that every spirit makes the decision to live or to end its life, and Cody, as tragic as it sounds, knew the timing wasn't right. His death helped us to prepare for Luke's death in some way, although never, at that time, did we think we would be attending the funerals of both our young sons.

It doesn't seem fair that their lives ended so quickly, but I know they will return to the physical plane one day, whether it is as our children or as someone else's.

Just For a Moment

Our hands have touched, our paths have crossed
A love is gained, a love is lost
Just for a moment I kissed the face
Of an innocent child I can't replace.

Just for a moment a maternal touch
Would say the words that meant so much
A soft caress, the gentle tears
That made those minutes last for years.

Just for a moment, I held your hand
My broken heart in your command
So much to tell you, so little time
Why were we punished, what was the crime?
They took part of me when they took you away
As much as I loved you, you weren't meant to stay
I gave you a hug that for always must last
As facing the future means leaving the past.

Our souls have merged, I live for you
Perhaps I'm living your life too
I will carry on; I can always stand tall
Because just for that moment, I had it all.

(BY NATALIE, IN MEMORY OF SAM DEAN ANTHONY)

The Hospital Experience

*T*HE PURPOSE OF THIS BOOK IS CERTAINLY NOT TO LAY blame on anyone. The purpose of sharing our stories is that it might help all of us—parents, friends, and family—to understand more fully the emotional consequences of losing a baby.

However, it is entirely reasonable that, following the death of a child, a parent will be plagued with questions of What if . . . ? and feelings of If only. . . . When questions and feelings of personal guilt run ceaselessly through your mind, it is likely that the issue of blame will arise. Some blame is often placed squarely at the feet of the medical profession, whether for an assumed malpractice or simply for an inadequacy in their levels of under-standing and compassion.

Peter and I will always believe that what happened to us could have been avoided. We will also always remember the lack of compassion shown us by the young doctors who delivered our twins and the absence of postnatal care I received once I had left the hospital. But we'll never know whether that belief or our per-ception of those events are based on fact or whether they are based on traumatic memories and unreasonable expectations. What I do know is that, either way, it's immaterial. We have been left with some bitterness and, at the end of the day, only we can address those feelings and attempt to overcome them.

Unfortunately, there are many men and women who harbor similar feelings, and they need to be able to voice their concerns in the same way that they need to be able to talk about their loss in a more general sense. I would not presume to comment on any of the stories shared with us in this chapter, to say whether those involved acted correctly or not and whether their actions were deliberate or accidental. They do need to be included, though, because while the medical professionals are undoubtedly becom-ing more aware and more capable in their dealings with parents, there is still some way to go.

One of the many wonderful people I spoke to while researching this book was Professor Michael Bennett, head of obstetrics and gynecology at the Royal Hospital for Women in Sydney. Thankfully, Michael and his wife, Jane, have no personal experience of the death of a child, but Michael, in his professional capacity, is all too aware of others' suffering. He wrote to me expressing his con-cern about the failure of the medical profession to understand the grief of parents in this situation and consequently their failure to provide adequately for the parents' emotional needs.

Apart from all the support Michael has given me in the writing of this book, for which I shall remain forever grateful, he gave me something far more important. He offered me the rare opportunity to address an audience of medical professionals; it was an opportunity to make a real difference by telling them a parent's point of view.

The following is an edited version of my address:

> In 1983, a psychologist named Herz published an article on the trauma of miscarriage, and she was overwhelmed with letters and telephone calls from readers who were anxious to express their suppressed feelings about their own experiences.
>
> "They were glad," she said, "that at long last this issue was being addressed."
>
> Nearly seventeen years later, my own published articles have been met by exactly the same response. Somehow, despite the frequency of miscarriage, both the medical profession and society in general are failing. We are allowing the aura of taboo that surrounds miscarriage to remain, and we are further entrenching what Professor Bennett and I refer to as the conspiracy of silence.
>
> One of the very first emotions of the grieving mother is guilt. This guilt makes it hard for women to be open about their grief, because they fear that the reaction of others might actually confirm that guilt. Her avoidance can and does encourage similar avoidance tactics by those around her. It's easier, after all, to say nothing than to find the right words.

Believe me, I know what I'm talking about. I have had several miscarriages, and I have suffered from both poor treatment by the medical profession and a lack of understanding and extraordinary ignorance on the part of others. Consequently I've made the decision to do what I can to change things: to raise awareness of the issue of miscarriage in order to help create a more supportive atmosphere in society, whereby both the man and the woman can draw on the strength of others.

Not too long after I arrived in Australia, my resolve in this decision was strengthened when an article appeared in one of the Sydney newspapers, entitled "Give It A Rest Commissioner." The columnist wrote how inappropriate he believed it was for me to have spoken publicly about my miscarriages. The thrust of his article was that this was a subject that should be kept within the confines of the home and family. It should not, he argued, be openly discussed.

I was at a loss to understand why. Is it so shameful to speak of losing a child? Should it be one of those things, like in Victorian England, that are never spoken about? I don't think so. With so many couples suffering the death or loss of a baby, I believe this should not be taboo, nor should it be swept under the carpet. What do we have to hide? As far as I'm concerned, the answer to that question is nothing, and this journalist, and people like him, should be made aware of that.

When a woman loses a baby at any stage of a pregnancy, it is almost inescapable that she will ask herself, What did I do? What could I have done differently? For the vast majority of us, the answer to both questions is nothing. But even though the weight of medical science tells us this, it's still very difficult to accept. In our hearts, it's extremely difficult to accept that we weren't at fault in some way.

I know of women who are intelligent, capable, well-read, but who still, after a miscarriage, have said things like "If only I hadn't continued to ride," or "I should never have carried on going to the gym." In our heads we know that that makes no sense at all, and that these things really make no difference. But it takes time to finally reach the point where we understand that—and to accept it. I think that we each go through a very important process. We embark on a search for answers, and during that search we learn about ourselves as individuals and as wives or husbands, and we learn about our family and friends, who become our essential nucleus of support.

Bearing all that in mind, I believe absolutely that it is essential to be able to speak to others, to express our emotions without fear of boring or shocking those who listen, and I also believe absolutely that members of the medical profession can play an extremely important part here. In most instances, it is men and women like you who will be the initial point of contact for the parents, and therefore it is you who must take responsibility for facilitating what is probably the most desperate need of the mother: to talk about what has happened. If you don't give the parents, and the mother particularly, this opportunity, then you take away the immediate chance for them to begin their search for answers and thereby to begin the grieving process without guilt or shame.

I know that it is difficult for anyone to fully understand the intensity of the emotions of others when they are suffering something you have no personal experience of. I also understand that your primary role is not that of counselor or psychologist, but it is so important for you to understand that to treat a miscarriage as a nonevent, because technically what has been lost was not a person but a fetus, to allow the woman to isolate herself and her distress by failing to actively encourage her to talk, is a great disservice to her. Not only may you be unintentionally confirming her guilt, you will most likely succeed only in perpetuating the conspiracy. If you, in the first instance, fail to acknowledge the extent of the loss, the chances are that the mother will internalize her emotions and will dwell on, nurture, and encourage those feelings of guilt and shame.

Banal platitudes such as "It's for the best," "It's nature's way," simply disempower the parents in their efforts to express the severity of their emotions. This grief, and its accompanying feelings of anger, shame, guilt, and depression, is a very real emotion, which, unless addressed, can result in the woman living with a sense of failure for many, many years. If you can offer her genuine sympathy and support, you will be telling her two things. First, and most important, that she is not to blame. Second, that it is entirely reasonable for her to question what has happened—for example, Why did it happen? Was it something I did? Was it something I didn't do? Will it happen again? —and to be given sound logical answers where they are available.

The death of one of your own children is one of life's greatest tragedies. It's a death that simply doesn't fall within the realm of our expectancy of life's pattern. When we talk about miscarriage, stillbirth, and neonatal death, what causes us the most pain is the failure of others, including friends, family, and those in the medical profession, to realize that, as far as the parents are concerned, our child has died.

I sincerely hope that those within the medical profession who read the following accounts of parental experiences will learn a very important lesson: acknowledge the extent of the parents' loss, and you will ease their pain and allow them to grieve without guilt or shame.

DONNA'S STORY

A FEW years ago, I had endometriosis, and after the operation, the doctors told me that I would probably find it hard to get pregnant. I was surprised, therefore, to find, several years later, that I was pregnant with identical twins.

When I got over the initial shock, I was so happy I couldn't wait for the big day to arrive. The doctor explained that because of my age I ought to have an amniocentesis, but with all the risks that seemed to be involved, we opted against it. He told us that instead we should go for an ultrasound, which we did, and they found there was a slight problem: one of the babies was bigger than the other. However, the technician said that this was quite common in twin pregnancies and there was no need for concern. We were told to go back two weeks later to check that everything was progressing okay.

There didn't seem to be anything to worry about, until suddenly another doctor called and asked us to come back straightaway. When we got there, he explained that because one of the babies was bigger than the other, we had no choice but to have some of the amniotic fluid removed. Apparently, if we didn't do this, there was a danger that I would go into premature labor and I would lose both twins.

As I lay on a bed, the doctor put a needle into my belly and took out a glassful of fluid. My husband said that as he watched the procedure, he could see that the doctor kept moving the needle around, and as he did so the hole was getting bigger and bigger. We didn't understand the repercussions of what he had done until we were on our way home and my water broke. My husband rushed me back to the hospital, and when we got there the nurse who was on duty simply said how sorry she was and told me to wait for the doctor.

I stayed in the hospital for four days, and each day they did another ultrasound and found that the babies' hearts were still beating. Everything seemed fine, even though I was losing more fluid. Then, on the fourth day, they couldn't find any heartbeats. They told us that both our babies had died, and I broke down and wept. I wanted to scream, because the pain in my heart was so unbearable. I felt so numb; I just couldn't believe that this could happen to me, especially as I thought I could still feel the babies moving. I was five months pregnant and all the doctor could say was he was sorry, he thought everything was going so well.

I had no choice then—I had to deliver the babies, but I had to wait for a few days for my cervix to soften. It was the worst few days of my life as I sat at home while my local priest joined us to pray for me, my family, and my babies. When I went back to the hospital, I made them do another ultrasound, because I was sure that I could feel the babies moving. They weren't; there were no little hands waving anymore.

They began to induce labor, and the following day, my first twin, the little one, was born and I named him Bailey. Two hours later, his brother Brock was born. My two little boys didn't even have a chance. We took the babies home with us, and in the car on the way back "Rock-a-bye" was playing on the radio. Whenever I hear that song, I get a pain in my heart and I think of my two boys. We buried them the next day next to my nan and pop, so they're with God now.

Every day I think about Bailey and Brock, and I wonder whether things would have been different if they hadn't taken the fluid from the sac. I guess I will never know, but if I could go back again, I would just let nature take its course.

Lisa's Story

I didn't get married until I was in my late thirties. Before then, I had occasionally thought about having a child as a single parent, but I didn't think it would be fair to the child, so I never did. Then, when I did get married, my husband, Ian, and I decided to try for a family straightaway, but we found that my tubes were blocked, so the only option was in vitro fertilization treatment. At the time, however, I felt that I must have been a big disappointment to Ian, and I felt so guilty that I couldn't give him the children he wanted so much. I even said, rather gingerly, one day that if he wanted to leave me, I would understand: I was thinking of the maxim "If you love someone, set them free." To my utter relief, he told me he had married me for me, not for the children we might or might not have.

I sometimes harbored thoughts of, What is this life all about if we can't have children? So, for me, there was never really any question of our not going onto the in vitro fertilization program. I knew when I started the treatment that there was only a 5 percent chance of success, so when I got pregnant on the first attempt, we were incredibly happy; this baby was just so precious.

I went for my first appointment with the obstetrician, but, unfortunately, I found him to be very cold, and I came away feeling unhappy about his taking care of my baby and me. However, a girlfriend told me that while he was cold and gruff, he was also actually very good, so I stayed with him.

My next appointment with him was to discuss treatment for bacteria found in my Pap smear. I was nervous about the possible side effects for my baby if I took antibiotics. As I said to the obstetrician, this was a very precious baby; my husband and I could not simply make love and have me get pregnant. I believe he never appreciated that fact, and all I got was a barrage of medical terms and words that went completely over my head, and I walked out with a prescription for an antibiotic ointment. Feeling unsure, I asked the pharmacist if I had made the right decision between tablets and ointment, and he just seemed to placate me. The bacteria was later put down as a possible contributing factor to the early birth of our son.

When I saw the obstetrician again, his attitude was much the same as before. I told him that I didn't want an amniocentesis, as I considered the risk to be too high. He was furious with me and gave me another barrage of medical terminology, again none of which I understood. I made an appointment to see my general practitioner, but he seemed to know less about amniocentesis than I did! I went to the library, searched the Internet, and tried to find out as much information as I could about the pros and cons of this invasive test, and it was frustrating how little there was. I felt there was pressure coming at me from all around to have the test because of my age, so at eighteen weeks I went ahead. Along with the bacteria, the amniocentesis was put down as a possible contributing factor to Callum's early birth.

Later in the pregnancy, at around twenty to twenty-one weeks, I started spotting, and as it got worse, I kept trying to contact the doctor. I called him four or five times, but he never returned my calls, until eventually, in desperation, I called the hospital and spoke to one of the nurses there. She called my doctor at home, and he then finally called me and told me to go and see him the following morning. When I got up the next day and was getting ready to go and see him, I suddenly had a huge blood loss. Luckily, my husband, who was working on shifts at the time, had just got home, and he rushed me straight to the hospital.

The doctor arrived, and in fact he then seemed to become quite caring. I suppose he knew my baby was probably going to die and therefore he finally felt some compassion. He put me on another course of antibiotics, and I lay on my side in bed, hoping the pregnancy could be saved. Four days later, I went into labor and my little boy was born, but he was too small, too premature for them to try to keep him alive. I learned later that if I had stayed pregnant for another week or two, then both Callum and I would have died, but I spent most of the next year wishing that I had died. They asked us if we wanted to name him, but we hadn't really thought about names yet. There were a couple we had discussed, nothing definite, but in the end we named him Callum.

We have foot- and handprints and we have a couple of photographs, although one of those is not very clear. We held him for the few minutes that he lived, his little heartbeat slowly diminishing as the tears rolled down our faces. We lost our son, and I knew then that we'd more than likely lost our chance to have a family.

The autopsy showed there was bacteria in the uterus and placenta; it had started up the umbilical cord. After my obstetrician had run through the report, he told me not to get pregnant again for at least six months and to take precautions. He still didn't seem to understand the situation! I believe that he was upset about what had happened, but I put the blame solely on him. I was paying him to look after my baby and me, but I do not believe he took due care. He certainly never appreciated how precious this pregnancy was to us.

The next day, before I left the hospital, we held Callum again and said goodbye. The emptiness in coming home was mortifying. I wanted to shrivel up and disappear, and I would lie in bed for hours crying, hoping if I lay there long enough I would die. I couldn't believe the acute pain of the grief I was feeling. I spent weeks blaming myself for what had happened, wondering whether maybe I shouldn't have hung out the washing—what was it I did wrong?

The phone rang constantly that first week, but I couldn't talk to anyone. It was about a week before I could talk to family and almost a month before I could talk to friends. Each time a bunch of flowers arrived, I would dissolve into tears, with those stabbing pains of grief wrenching at my body. Ian would always be there holding and cuddling me until I stopped.

I found that everyone kept asking me when I was going back to work, until eventually I began to think I must have been being melodramatic and pathetic. After just two weeks, and even before my son's funeral, I went back, but with hindsight I realize it was an insane thing to do. I was still mummified: I could barely talk, I didn't want anyone to look at me, I felt I was on the edge. To make matters worse, I got all the usual platitudes from people, such as, "Oh well, these things happen" and "Oh well, you'll try again, won't you?" I was thankful when someone simply said, "I am sorry about what happened."

Professional help didn't seem very forthcoming. The hospital social worker took two days to return my call, and the first grief counselor I spoke to told me she was stopping counseling. I then had to wait several weeks before someone else called me, and meanwhile I felt so lonely and isolated. I had started to build a brick wall around myself, and I was guarded about what I said to anyone, as I realized that no one had an understanding of the grief I felt. The help is out there, but you have to go and get it. The problem is, with the depression that sets in after child loss, you really want it to come to you. I guess that is why, to a large extent, I am still struggling with Callum's death, why I'm still very angry, and why I still believe it should never have happened.

In vitro fertilization treatment is usually stopped once a woman reaches forty-two. I'm forty-two now, but they're allowing me to keep trying for a short while because, having become pregnant the first time, I'm a good candidate. Sadly, the last four tries have failed, and in my heart I now know that I'll never be a mother. It's so sad. My husband and I would love to have a child, and he would make such a wonderful father—children adore him.

It is now over a year since Callum died, and not a day goes by when I don't think of him. I still cry often, and Ian still holds me until the tears stop. A part of me died with Callum, but despite the torrid and horrendous experience of child loss, I would not want to change anything. If I hadn't had Callum, I would never have experienced that deep love that a mother has for her child. I have kept his ashes, as it is my responsibility to look after my child—one day they will be scattered with mine at our favorite beach. We always had hopes and dreams that Callum would live to enjoy and love that beach as much as we do.

DEBORAH'S STORY

IN 1991, when I was seven months pregnant with my second child, I got a very bad dose of flu, and a week later I started to pass blood. My general practitioner was obviously concerned, because he arranged for me to be admitted to the hospital immediately, but when I got there, no one talked to me about what was going on or what they were going to do for me.

Six days I lay in the hospital bed as the bleeding got worse. Every night I would have contractions that would last from 6:00 P.M. to 6:00 A.M., but nothing was ever done about them. The bleeding continued until finally I started to hemorrhage, but when the doctor arrived and I asked him what was happening, he just looked at me and told me my baby was going to die. I knew that the hospital I was in could not accommodate a premature baby, but when I asked if they could transfer me to Sydney, they said it wasn't necessary. Throughout all of this, my baby was still active and his heartbeat was strong, so they seemed to think there was no need for them to do anything other than leave me resting.

Early one morning, my waters broke, and I knew right away that this was it. I immediately told the nurses and asked them to get the doctor, but they told me I'd have to wait until he did his rounds at 7:00 A.M. I could feel the contractions coming strong and often, but although I continually buzzed for help, no one came. Eventually, at 6:00 A.M., my little boy arrived, and I remember looking at him; his head and one shoulder were blue, and I could see that the cord was around his neck. By this stage, I was completely hysterical and kept ringing for a nurse, but still no one came. After about twenty minutes, a nurse finally came into the room. She looked at me and at the baby lying between my legs and then she covered us both in a sheet and walked out of the room. Ten minutes later, she came back and took my little boy from me, wrapping him in a plastic sheet as if he were vegetable scraps. She did speak to me while she was doing this, but I have no idea what she said, and one and a half hours after I gave birth to my little boy, the hospital discharged me and sent me home.

Through my own research, I found out what had happened. As a result of the flu, I had abruptio placentae, whereby my antibodies attacked the placenta, causing it to shred away from the wall of the uterus.

I have spent the last eight years carrying the guilt of that day, wishing that I had attempted mouth-to-mouth resuscitation or something, anything to have kept him alive, but I had no medical experience or knowledge. Although my baby was born at

6:05 A.M., and the friend who was with me can verify that, the birth certificate shows his time of birth as 7:30 A.M. My attempts to sue the hospital later failed when the lawyers told us we were never going to win, as no one in the hospital was prepared to admit to the mistakes they had made.

Ultimately, my relationship with my son's father broke down. He couldn't understand my grief and expected me to get over it, but you don't "get over it." It's with you all the time, no matter what else happens in your life.

I already had a son, Luke, who was thirteen when we lost Jordan, and he was equally traumatized by what happened. In September 1998, I gave birth to my precious daughter, Hayley Rose. She is a total delight, and she has helped to heal my broken heart.

SHIRLEEN'S STORY

IN AUGUST 1996, I went for the last antenatal checkup with my doctor. I had not felt the baby move since the day before, and I was worried, especially as my first two pregnancies had ended in miscarriage. For me, those fears were very real, but the doctor thought I was being silly and went about examining me in what I thought was a rather rough way. Then he turned to me and said, "I'm sorry. I know how much you wanted this baby." At first the words didn't register, and then suddenly it hit me—our baby had died.

I had gone on my own to the hospital, so I had to drive myself home to get some extra clothes and then return to the hospital later that day. I can't even remember driving the twelve and a half miles, because I was frightened and confused and crying so much. The hospital had called my husband, but they hadn't told him what had happened, so he thought I was in labor and arrived at the hospital excited and full of anticipation. Together with my parents, we watched in hope as they did an ultrasound, praying that they had made some kind of terrible mistake. But they hadn't. Looking at the screen, it was obvious my baby had died.

I can still remember the staff offering my husband and me a roast beef lunch and offering sandwiches to my parents, who were in the room outside. It was as if nothing of any significance had happened and we were expected to just get on with life, eat food, and forget. The only other thing we had to make a decision about was whether I wanted to keep the baby inside me for a few more weeks or whether I wanted them to induce labor. We decided to have labor induced, and after a long and difficult labor, Jessica Edna was born.

My memories of my beautiful daughter are with me every day. I have a piece of her hair in a locket my friends gave me, and I wear it around my neck always. We also have some photographs, which I treasure. We visit her lovely little grave often. I take pink flowers and baby's breath, which she never had, and I always feel an incredible sadness and a longing for what might have been. I now have two wonderful daughters, and I can't imagine life without them. When they are asleep, I find myself constantly looking at them and touching their little faces to check that they are still breathing. When they are old enough to understand, I will tell them all about their "big" sister: she is the bright star that shines over their bedrooms.

LARAINE'S STORY

MY HUSBAND and I were overjoyed when it was confirmed that I was pregnant, and when they did the first ultrasound, the baby looked fine, with a good strong heartbeat. Everything was great, until at fourteen weeks I developed a urinary tract infection. The doctor prescribed medication that, unbeknown to me, contained penicillin, a drug I'm very allergic to. My medical records folder had the words "Allergic to penicillin, do not prescribe" written all over the front in red letters, so I had no need to think he would not heed the warning.

The infection eventually cleared, but meanwhile I had developed a rash all over my upper body, and it was still there when I went for my next checkup. When I got there, I was stunned to have the doctor ask me if I was sure I was pregnant, as he could find no signs of a pregnancy. The chief gynecologist then came and confirmed that I was no longer pregnant and explained to me that sometimes, when the fetus dies, the body reabsorbs it. Apparently, this is what must have happened to me, although they assured me that the medication was not the cause. I was so shocked by what they were telling me, I could barely explain to my husband what had happened.

Two months later, after I'd lost a lot of blood, they found that some of the dead material was still inside me, so I was then subjected to a dilation and curettage. For months afterwards, I suffered from crippling lower abdominal pain, until I finally passed a large clot. I was taken to the emergency unit at the local hospital, and the doctor there told me that there was no doubt that the penicillin I had been given caused the death of my baby. He also told me that, of course, it could never be proved.

When I became pregnant again, all was well until at twelve weeks, I began to bleed. Once again I went into the hospital, and, sadly, I miscarried this baby as well. I went into shock, and all I can remember is feeling so cold and shaking uncontrollably. The nurses seemed to be rushing around and doing things to me like putting on an oxygen mask. For the second time, we were absolutely devastated, and like many women, I blamed myself. It was only later that I came to terms with the fact that I actually wasn't to blame.

A year later, we decided to try again, but this time it wasn't so easy to get pregnant. Finally, though, I did get pregnant, and although I worried all the way through the pregnancy, we became the proud parents of a beautiful daughter. We were then told not to try for any more children, because the risks involved were too great, so my husband had a vasectomy.

As my daughter grew up, she would often ask why she didn't have any brothers or sisters, so when she was old enough to understand, we told her about the miscarriages. She is now seventeen years old, and we thank God every day for her.

I often wonder how the children we lost would have looked and what sort of people they would have become. Their loss is something I will never get over; children are such precious God-given gifts, and we are so lucky to have them.

JUNE'S STORY

IN THE past, I always felt sorry for women who suffered miscarriages, and I tried to say the right consoling words. It was only recently, however, that I felt the anguish and devastation firsthand, and it was this that helped my husband and me to truly feel empathy for the couples who are presented with this life tragedy.

It was late one Friday afternoon when I first started spotting. I called my husband and asked him to come home immediately to look after our nineteen-month-old child, and I took myself down to the hospital. After a long wait to be attended to and a great deal of walking about while I filled in the mandatory paperwork, I was eventually informed by a doctor that I had a bladder infection. He openly admitted he had little experience with maternity cases, but even so, he didn't call in another doctor or obstetrician and he didn't ask that an ultrasound be carried out for a more accurate account of what was happening to me. Instead, I was sent home with orders to rest and to take antibiotics.

By Saturday, I had convinced myself I was having a miscarriage. As the bleeding continued all day and through the night, I eventually called the hospital, where the nursing staff told me to "take it easy."

By Sunday, the bleeding was very heavy, and two more visits to the hospital found them seemingly undisturbed as the tragedy unfolded before them and my blood pressure rose. I received nothing more than repeated instructions to "take it easy," until finally, on Sunday night, I managed to be seen by a doctor who was visiting from another hospital. He immediately ordered an ultrasound, and sadly they found my baby had died at twelve weeks. Then, to compound the grief I felt at this loss, I was placed near the maternity ward. The staff were thoughtful enough to put me in a bed as far away from the labor ward as possible, but I could still hear newborns crying and nurses discussing the births. It was like driving a knife into my heart.

From that moment on, I received a barrage of well-meaning but useless and often hurtful information and comments. All the usual platitudes, such as "It's nature's way," "It was probably for the best," and our personal favorite, guaranteed to trivialize the anguish, "You can always have another one." If we do eventually have another child, he or she will be number three; our second child has died, and there will never be a way—or another human being—to replace him or her.

Of course, there have also been some wonderful people who have helped us. One of the nurses in the hospital shared her personal experience with me, and other people have come out of the woodwork to also share their stories. They seem to be the only people who truly understand our pain. There were two people from my church who came up and just hugged me. That was a great comfort, as it appeared they understood that the pain is too great to try and ease with any words.

We learned an important lesson during this time: how easy it is to forget that the father has also suffered a severe loss. There were few who thought to offer him consolation. We expect dads to take such a big part in labor, night feedings, and parenting generally, but we conveniently forget them when they need support.

The way in which doctors treated me tends only to add to our grief. I don't necessarily believe any medical intervention could have saved our second child. However, what I am appalled at is the lack of any sense of urgency I received. Had the same concern and intervention been given on Friday afternoon that was afforded me on Sunday night, the devastating result might have been the same, but we would have been spared more than forty-eight hours of unnecessary emotional turmoil.

I also discovered that my grief was all-inclusive. In a sense, I grieved over everything to do with the baby: unworn maternity clothes, the empty crib, not knowing what our child looked like or the baby's sex, not having a burial or a coffin. But my husband and I have found a memorial for our child that is meaningful to both of us and that has helped us with the grieving process. We have put together a box of items full of memories and symbols of our second baby. These mementos are representative of our much loved child, and they help us deal with the grief because they are tangible. We can see and feel these items, unlike the child whom we won't get to hold until one day when we are reunited in Heaven.

Saying Goodbye

You seemed so full of life
Not ready to succumb to one more trial
Stretching out your legs
So eager to experience life
But your tiny body was not able
To rail against your situation
We know that releasing you was right
But it doesn't help to ease the pain of your loss
We had hoped you could live for your brother
Showing the promise he could not fulfill
But instead you were granted just three weeks more
Saying goodbye on the same day, almost to the hour
Almost as if in union with your brother.

Life is too delicate
The loss of one was so hard
But now the loss of another does not seem real
For how can we grieve any more?
All that is left is numbness
A feeling that life could be so hard
So grieve for the fallen brothers
Who were dealt a hand that would fold too quickly.

(BY NIGEL, IN MEMORY OF ETHAN AND BAILEY)

The Future

ITHOUT EXCEPTION, THE WOMEN AND MEN I have spoken to expressed a sense of frustration when faced with the comment "It was nature's way," and that's understandable. Knowing that there was some fundamental problem with our baby's physical development doesn't make our loss any easier to bear. Unfortunately, in the majority of cases where miscarriage occurs before the twelfth week, the truth is that it is in fact "nature's way." For this reason, except perhaps where a woman suffers recurrent early miscarriages, little can or should be done in terms of medical intervention and research. This is something we quite simply have to accept—and something most women do accept when they go on to have healthy, full-term pregnancies.

For miscarriages and stillbirths that occur later in pregnancy, however, the explanation is rarely so simple. To date, relatively little research has been conducted into what those causes are, and without that research, it is very difficult to prevent or minimize the risk of this tragedy. That said, some research is being carried out in various centers around the world, and it is wonderful to note that enormous headway has been made in certain areas. The issue of spontaneous premature labor is one area where new and exciting discoveries are being made, and it is with much gratitude to Professor Roger Smith that I am able to share some of those discoveries.*

According to Professor Smith, between six and eight percent of all pregnancies end prematurely—that is, after twenty weeks and before thirty-seven weeks—and, of those, perhaps half are a result of spontaneous premature labor. The gestation period for the "viability" of a prematurely delivered baby has dropped significantly in the last decade or so as doctors have become increasingly skilled at saving these little babies. But there still are no guarantees that a baby will survive; indeed many of them do not,

*Roger Smith is professor of endocrinology at the University of Newcastle and John Hunter Hospital in New South Wales. He earned his medical degree from the University of Sydney in 1975. After receiving a doctorate in neuroendocrinology at St. Bartholomew's Hospital in London, he returned to Australia in 1981 to join what was then a new medical school at Newcastle. In 1989, he established the Mothers and Babies Research Center, which emphasizes investigations into the endocrinology of parturition.

and when they do they may be afflicted by difficulties such as cerebral palsy, intellectual handicaps, and breathing problems.

The problem so far has been that scientists have had little understanding of the biological mechanism that controls birth timing and thus of how to keep that mechanism from operating inappropriately. Professor Smith and his colleagues have set out, therefore, to develop a greater understanding of this, so that premature labor can be prevented or at least delayed until the baby has a much higher chance of survival outside the womb.

The key word when we are talking about birth timing is *parturition*. This refers to the uterine, cervical, and other changes that make labor possible and that usually take place in the last two weeks of pregnancy. Recent research has afforded a much clearer sense of the controls on birth timing, a deciphering of how parturition is controlled. What Professor Smith and researchers in other centers have found could be referred to as a "battle of the hormones": that is, progesterone and estrogen. A successful pregnancy without premature labor depends on the correct balance of hormone levels in the mother's body at any given time during her pregnancy.

Progesterone is a steroid hormone secreted by the placenta into the mother's circulation from the early stages of pregnancy, and its function is to prepare and maintain the uterus for pregnancy. The structural features of a pregnancy—the uterus, a relaxed bag of disconnected smooth muscle cells; the cervix, the tightly closed ring that seals the bottom of the uterus; and the tough collagen fibers that keep the cervix firm and inflexible—are all maintained by progesterone. The placenta also secretes estrogen, another steroid hormone, which opposes progesterone and promotes contractions. A successful pregnancy depends on the balance of hormonal power remaining with progesterone until around the thirty-seventh or thirty-eighth week. The shift in this balance of power should ideally be gradual, as the estrogen levels rise only slowly throughout the pregnancy. When, ultimately, the power base shifts to estrogen, parturition begins, and the mother's body prepares itself for labor.

When the estrogen level rises sufficiently, the muscle cells of the uterus, which until then have been disconnected, begin to synthesize a protein called connexin. Protein molecules form junctions that electrically link one muscle cell to another, and it is this linking that enables the wall of the uterus to contract, initially in what we know as Braxton Hicks contractions, and finally for the purpose of labor itself.

Other hormones and chemicals promoted by the rise in estrogen levels work toward increasing the force of the contractions and the digestion of the collagen fibers, thereby making the cervix more malleable so that it can dilate and finally open. In the baby itself, hormones that encourage the correct development of the lungs also develop.

The discovery of these facts provided researchers with an extraordinary insight into the process of human pregnancy, but one important piece of information continued to elude them: the nature of the switch, in the fetus or in the mother, that activates placental estrogen secretion. Finding the answer was both practically and ethically difficult to do through close study of humans, and the clues came in the end from experiments conducted on other large mammals, especially sheep. By the mid-1980s, studies had discovered the basic regulatory mechanism in sheep and also discerned that the same mechanism exists in most mammals.

It was found that somewhere around the middle of the sheep's gestation period, a series of hormonal changes occur that lead to a shift in the balance of progesterone and estrogen. The fetal brain begins to secrete a hormone called the corticotropin-releasing hormone (CRH), which in turn encourages the secretion of the adrenocorticotropic hormone (ACTH) into the fetal circulation, instructing the adrenal gland to make cortisol. It is cortisol that then activates enzymes in the placenta that convert progesterone to estrogen. As the cortisol level rises, it facilitates the maturing of the lungs as well as shifting the balance of power until the progesterone level is low enough for parturition to start.

Having pieced together this process, researchers were disappointed to discover that in the case of humans, where cortisol does indeed encourage the maturation of the lungs—women threatening premature labor are often given cortisol injections for this purpose—it does not affect parturition. Further investigations produced evidence suggesting that most CRH in humans comes from the placenta, as opposed to the fetal brain in the case of sheep. The pathway toward parturition is therefore markedly different.

Various medical teams throughout the world studied the link between CRH and parturition. Studies conducted in England and the United States during the late 1980s found that women who went into premature labor had higher blood levels of CRH at the time of delivery than did women tested at the same week of pregnancy who did not deliver prematurely.

At around this time, Mark McLean, a doctoral student working with Professor Smith, began his thesis based on far more rigorous testing for the possible links between CRH and the onset of parturition. McLean's project took several years to complete and involved taking regular blood samples from nearly five hundred women throughout their pregnancies. Finally, in the mid-1990s, the results were ready for analysis. They confirmed that CRH levels increase as gestation advances and discovered that the levels actually rise exponentially throughout pregnancy. The most exciting discovery, however, was the fact that maternal CRH levels taken at sixteen to twenty weeks of pregnancy roughly predicted when a woman would give birth. The higher those levels, the more likely it was that the mother would go into premature labor; the lower the levels, the more likely it was that the mother would go past her due date.

McLean had uncovered the presence of a "placental clock," which appeared to be set in early pregnancy and which controlled the speed at which the pregnancy advanced. His discovery offered the possibility of identifying women at risk of premature spontaneous labor by measuring CRH levels early in pregnancy.

There is still some way to go with this discovery. Analyses of CRH are not yet done routinely, in part because the best methods for measurement and the most useful time to perform the tests are still under evaluation. Also, it must not be forgotten that there are other causes of premature labor, such as infection of the baby. But overall, what Professor Smith, his team at Newcastle, and the teams at research centers throughout the world have given us is a substantial ray of hope for the future.

Today, research into the many causes of miscarriage and still-birth is ongoing. Most of it is very much in its infancy and therefore could not be included here, but we should be heartened to know that these men and women are working tirelessly in their respective fields of expertise. Their endeavors hold promise for achieving a very precious goal: giving more babies the chance to realize their full potential and more couples the chance to realize their dreams.

Searching for Your Baby

WHILE THERE REMAINS A GREAT RELUCTANCE to talk openly about the loss of a baby, and there certainly remains in society generally an inability to deal adequately with the emotions of the parents who experience miscarriage and stillbirth, we are at least fortunate today to know that when this tragedy does strike, there is a growing recognition by the professionals of our need, as parents, to say goodbye to our baby.

Years ago, no such recognition existed. For the most part, it was believed better for the mother not to see her child, not to hold her child, and especially not to know what became of her child once the baby died. In fact, any involvement with the baby was actively discouraged, and the parents were shielded from what was regarded as unnecessary grief.

Scattered throughout the world are cemeteries where areas have been dedicated to the burial, in unmarked graves, of those little babies. Also scattered throughout the world are parents who have no knowledge of their babies' whereabouts and who therefore have no place to lay their flowers.

Many of the women who wrote to me about their experiences of decades ago expressed a desire to know where their baby was, but each was at a loss as to how to go about the search. For that reason, I have included guidelines for parents who wish to bring some resolution to their grief by finding their lost child. My heartfelt thanks go to the Department of Social Work at the Royal Hospital for Women in Sydney, Australia, for the following information.

WHAT DO YOU WANT TO KNOW?

SOME PARENTS are unsure about exactly what information they want to obtain. Some have certain information already, while others will be starting with nothing except the date, time, and place of their baby's birth. Before you embark on your search, ask yourself what it is you want to know. It is important that you be clear about how much, or how little, information would benefit you in your quest. Some women begin with very hazy information—it may be hard to recall clearly what happened, or they may have been ill at the time of the birth and were unable to discuss it with their partner. Even if you can't remember the exact details, don't let it put you off trying.

The questions you might want answers to are:

- Where is my baby now?
- Are there any tangible mementos of him or her?
- Is there any documentation relating to the birth in existence?
- What actually happened while I was in the hospital?
- Why did my baby die?
- Did the hospital staff do everything that could have been reasonably expected of them?

WHERE TO BEGIN

MEDICAL RECORDS:

Under the Freedom of Information Act, you are entitled to see any medical records relating to all your visits and admissions to the hospital. You will be charged a processing fee to obtain the information, and you should apply, in writing, to the medical records department at the hospital where you had your baby.

Before the records department staff can forward you a copy of your medical records, they will need to know

- your name at the time of your baby's birth
- your address at the time
- your date of birth

Although your medical records will appear in a rather clinical and impersonal format, it is important to bear in mind that the contents are likely to invoke many sad and long-suppressed memories for you. There will be things that you may have forgotten and things you may not have even known, which may sadden you and perhaps give rise to more questions. But having this information in front of you, discovering things you were unaware of, or clarifying knowledge that was previously a hazy memory for you is all-important. In the first instance, it may well set you back on the emotional roller coaster from years gone by, but that is undoubtedly a good thing. Revisiting the pain in this way enables you to reevaluate and reassess your experience and to reorder previously jumbled or inaccurate memories.

However beneficial this first step of discovery might ultimately be, professionals strongly recommend that you read over your records in the presence of a supportive friend, a member of your family, or a professional.

BIRTH AND DEATH CERTIFICATES:

Whether or not birth and death certificates exist is very much dependent on where and when your baby was born. The legislation governing the requirement to register the birth and death of a baby varies from country to country, from state to state, and from year to year.

It will be necessary for you to make contact with your local registry of births, deaths, and marriages in order to determine the legislation applicable to the birth of your baby, and the existence or otherwise of any certificate of record. Where there is a certificate, it will be issued to you for a fee following a written application.

As an example, the following information details the changes in New South Wales, Australia law defining stillbirth and the requisite registration of the birth and death of a baby:

- **1935–1969:** Stillbirth was defined as the death of a baby of twenty-eight weeks' gestation (seven months) or over and included any baby not born alive who measured at least fourteen inches in length. The baby's birth and death were both registered, and certificates can be requested.

- **1969–1992:** A stillborn baby was one of at least twenty weeks' gestation or at least 14 ounces who had not breathed at delivery. Registration of the birth and death were prohibited and the information was recorded as an index item only.

- **1992–1995:** A stillborn baby was one of at least 14 ounces at delivery or at least twenty weeks' gestation who had not breathed since delivery. The birth and death were registered and certificates issued. The 1992 amendment to the act had an important retrospective clause: you could register the birth of a baby who was stillborn during the years 1969–1992 as a "prenatal record," even though registration was not permitted at the time.

- **JANUARY 1996 TO THE PRESENT:** A stillborn baby is one who exhibits no sign of respiration or heartbeat after birth and is of at least twenty weeks' gestation (or at least 14 ounces if the gestation period is unclear). Births and deaths are now required to be registered and certificates are then issued.

ADDITIONAL INFORMATION:

Parents whose baby was born at a time when the registration of birth and death was not required have a more arduous task. The social worker at the hospital where your baby was born may be able to help you in your search and even arrange for you to talk to a medical professional about your medical records if you would like some of the terminology explained to you.

Alternatively, you can determine—according to your religion and the location of the hospital where your baby was born—the most likely cemetery where the hospital would have arranged for your baby to be buried. Call them; the men and women who work in these areas are very aware of the increasing need for parents to find their babies, and many of them work hard to ensure that your efforts are successful. They understand how traumatic the search process is for you.

One of the hardest things for parents to learn is that their baby was not accorded the sort of funeral and final resting place they would have arranged had they been given the opportunity. The terrible reality is that most of those babies who died many years ago were buried in multiple and unmarked graves. Some cemetery records will be able to tell you exactly where your baby is buried, some will only be able to give you a general indication of the location, and others will have no information at all. Missing or incomplete information will obviously be distressing for you, but don't give up; the vast majority of parents who set out on this difficult journey are rewarded in the end and find some inner peace and a long-awaited resolution to their emotional turmoil.

If, despite all your efforts, you are unfortunate in your search, please bear in mind that there are other ways in which you can focus your grief and other tangible ways in which you can remember your baby. Many cemeteries, for example, have created or are creating special gardens of remembrance for our babies, areas where memorials can be established and where parents can simply go to be near their baby.

Finally, on a more personal note, many of us eventually find ways in which to commemorate the children we have lost. Some of us have precious photographs that we keep on display, some of us plant trees or bushes that, with each passing year, symbolize the growth our children would have enjoyed had they lived. Others have cards, photographs, and letters that are kept locked away but that can be taken out when the need to remember arises. My own memories are locked away in a small metal box; I know they're there, and very occasionally I take them out for a few private moments of grief. A copy of this book will soon join those other memories. You might consider creating your own memorial or form of acknowledgement for your baby, such as

- planting a tree or shrub in your baby's memory
- creating a memorial certificate or memento booklet of drawings and writings
- placing a notice in the newspaper recognizing your baby's birth and death (some friends of mine do this every year to celebrate their daughter's birthday)

- including your baby's name, as a sibling, on subsequent children's birth certificates
- holding a religious ceremony
- laying a plaque at your local cemetery or garden of remembrance

Each of you will know when you reach your journey's end, but however far you manage—or choose—to travel, I wish you well.

Glossary of Medical Terms

ANY OF THE STORIES IN THIS BOOK TALK ABOUT medical conditions that will be unfamiliar to some readers. For his assistance in explaining these terms in such a way as to be easily understood, I am indebted once again to Professor Michael Bennett. The list below is as comprehensive as we were able to make it. If there are other conditions or terms that you do not understand, I urge you to contact your own doctor. Ask him or her to set some time aside to answer your questions, and have a list of questions ready before you meet, to ensure that you don't forget an important issue.

ABRUPTIO PLACENTAE

In this condition, the placenta, which is normally sited in the uterus, partially detaches from the uterine wall, resulting in loss of blood, some of which may exit through the vagina. The condition may result in fetal death, in the onset of labor, or in the placenta functioning less well, since it is partially separated from the maternal circulation. Alternatively, there may be no discernible effects. This condition is almost always associated with pain, whereas bleeding from a placenta previa is painless.

AMNIOCENTESIS

This is the technique whereby a needle is inserted, under ultrasound control, through the mother's abdomen into the uterus, avoiding both the fetus and the placenta. A sample of amniotic fluid is withdrawn, and the fetal cells are cultured in order to obtain the chromosome makeup of the baby. This technique, as with chorionic villus sampling, increases the risk of miscarriage by 0.5 percent and classically is offered to women who are thirty-six years and older or who have an increased risk of having a baby with a chromosome malformation. The laboratory process of culture and analysis of the chromosomes usually takes two to three weeks.

ANTEPARTUM HEMORRHAGE

This term refers to vaginal bleeding occurring after twenty weeks of pregnancy.

ANTIPHOSPHOLIPID SYNDROME

Some 15 percent of women with recurrent pregnancy loss are found to have antiphospholipid antibodies of one sort or another. These antibodies are primarily responsible for thrombosis in a variety of vessels and can also occur in men. Women with the antiphospholipid syndrome who are not treated by means of an anticoagulant have a very high risk of recurrent miscarriage.

CHORIONIC VILLUS SAMPLING

A sample of the developing placenta is obtained at about the eleventh week of pregnancy by either introducing a needle through the abdomen and advancing it to the edge of the placenta under ultrasound guidance or by passing a very fine catheter up through the cervix and into the uterus, again to the edge of the placenta. A sample of tissue is sucked into a syringe, and the chromosome makeup of this tissue is determined in the laboratory following culture of the cells. The chromosome makeup of this tissue almost always reflects the chromosome makeup of the embryo. The procedure increases the risk of miscarriage by approximately 0.5 percent.

CORPUS LUTEUM CYST

A cyst is simply a structure containing a liquid. In the first half of the menstrual cycle, there is a follicle that, after ovulation and the changes brought about by the hormonal circulation, becomes a cystic structure called a corpus luteum. There are almost never symptoms or problems associated with it.

CYSTIC FIBROSIS

This is a hereditary disease affecting the mucus-secreting and sweat glands. It is the most common potentially lethal disorder in Caucasians, with as many as one in twenty-two people being a carrier. Recent discoveries in medical science now enable doctors to identify both carriers and affected infants, and treatment has improved to a point where at least 50 percent of sufferers are still alive at the age of twenty-five. Previously, death in infancy and childhood was common. Repeated respiratory tract infections and chronic lung disease, as well as an inability of the intestines to function normally, are characteristic of this condition.

Diaphragmatic Hernia

The diaphragm is the muscle separating the abdominal cavity from the thoracic cavity, and its movement up and down assists breathing. As a result of a developmental failure, sometimes a portion of the muscle sheet is absent, and the abdominal cavity and the chest cavity are connected. Abdominal contents, such as bowel, stomach, and even liver, may enter the chest through this hole (hernia), and by their presence severely restrict the development of fetal lungs. These babies require surgery immediately after birth so that the hole may be closed; otherwise death is inevitable.

Embryo

This term is restricted to a fertilized ovum up to the age of ten weeks.

Fetus

The later developmental stages of the embryo, from the end of the tenth week up until the time of birth.

Group B Streptococcal Infection

Group B streptococcal organisms are found in the vagina in 20 percent of women. The infection causes no specific symptoms, but the fetus may contract it as it passes down the birth canal. Usually no problem arises, but very rarely—one in 10,000 cases—serious and even fatal consequences do occur.

Klinefelter's Syndrome

This is a condition affecting males, caused by an abnormal

chromosome complement, usually an extra X chromosome. The male is typically tall, his puberty is delayed, and he has a small penis and testes. Even if they are able to develop a full sexual relationship, these men are infertile.

MISCARRIAGE

This term refers to the loss of an embryo or fetus before twenty weeks' gestation.

NECROTIZING ENTEROCOLITIS (NEC)

This is an ischemic (meaning a lack of blood supply) and inflammatory disease of the bowel, of unknown cause; it occurs predominantly in premature infants. It is a serious illness, with significant mortality and morbidity rates, and because an operation may be necessary, the infant should be managed jointly by a neonatal pediatrician and a pediatric surgeon as soon as the diagnosis is made.

NEONATAL DEATH

This term refers to a baby that is born alive at between twenty and forty weeks' gestation but that dies within forty-two days of birth.

PLACENTA PREVIA

In this condition, the placenta is implanted, either partially or wholly, in the lower uterine segment and lies below the presenting part of the fetus. The extent may be minor, in which case vaginal birth is possible, or major, in which case a cesarean section is required.

POSTERIOR URETHRAL VALVE

This is a condition affecting male fetuses only. An obstruction to the outflow of urine from the bladder, caused by two semi-circular membranous valves, results in distention of the urinary tract and bladder. A significant number of babies with this condition also have other abnormalities, and permanent kidney damage is common.

POTTER'S SYNDROME

This syndrome results from the absence of amniotic fluid, frequently caused by the failure of development of the kidneys. The baby can have a number of physical malformations, including cysts on the kidneys and lungs, an underdeveloped jaw, no bladder, and no anus.

STILLBIRTH

This term refers to a baby born dead between twenty and forty weeks' gestation.

TROPHOBLASTIC DISEASE— MOLAR PREGNANCY

This is the name given to an unusual spectrum of benign and malignant tumors that are derived from part of the human placenta. These tumors secrete human chorionic gonadotrophin (HCG), the first hormone tested for to determine pregnancy. Not only does this hormone provide the signs and symptoms of pregnancy, but it is a very sensitive marker that correlates well with the progression of the condition and is therefore very helpful in assessing treatment.

ASSISTED REPRODUCTIVE TECHNIQUES

GAMETE INTRA-FALLOPIAN TRANSFER (GIFT)

This is the introduction of both ovum and fresh sperm into the outer portion of the fallopian tube, in the hope that fertilization will take place and result in an intrauterine pregnancy. The technique was developed in order to avoid the religious objections to in vitro fertilization.

IN VITRO FERTILIZATION (IVF)

This is the fertilization of an ovum in a laboratory. The subsequent embryo may then either be frozen or transferred back to the woman's uterus in an attempt to achieve pregnancy. The technique was originally developed for women with blocked tubes, and because fertilization occurs in a laboratory, the babies are often called test-tube babies. The first such birth occurred in 1978.

INTRA-CYTOPLASMIC SPERM INJECTION (ICSI)

This is the injection of a single sperm into the ovum, thus fertilizing it. The technique has revolutionized the treatment of men with severely low sperm counts.

INTRA-UTERINE INSEMINATION (IUI)

In this procedure, sperm are transferred by catheter into the uterus in order to overcome problems in the cervix in females and impotence or retrograde ejaculation into the bladder in males.

PRONUCLEAR STAGE TRANSFER (PROST)

This technique begins with in vitro fertilization, but whereas that process transfers the fertilized egg to the uterus, with Pronuclear Stage Transfer the egg is transferred to the fallopian tube.

Bereavement Support Contact List

THE FOLLOWING LIST COMPRISES PEOPLE AND organizations that specialize in supporting parents during the traumatic period following miscarriage and stillbirth. These people frequently offer a lifeline for men and women who need to talk but find it difficult to do so openly with those close to them. The list is by no means exhaustive, but it will hopefully make a good start.

If you are fortunate enough to have access to the Internet, do consider using it. I have been amazed at the level of resources available there, including several sites dedicated to the issue of parenthood and bereavement.

UNITED STATES

AIDING A MOTHER AND FATHER
EXPERIENCING NEONATAL DEATH
(A.M.E.N.D.)
1559 Villa Rosa
Hazelwood, MO 63042
Tel: (314) 291-0892

BEREAVED PARENTS USA
P.O. Box 95
Park Forest, IL 60466
Fax: (708) 748-9184

BEREAVEMENT CENTER
Jewish Family and Children's
Services
2150 Post Street
San Francisco, CA 94115
Tel: (415) 449-3808

BEREAVEMENT SUPPORT SERVICES AND
COPE/OUTREACH DEPARTMENT—
NOMOTC
P.O. Box 23188
Albuquerque, NM 87192-1188
Tel: (505) 275-0955
Fax: (505) 296-1863
www.nomotc.org

CENTERING CORPORATION
1531 West Saddle Creek Road
Omaha, NE 68104-5064
Tel: (402) 553-1200

CENTER FOR LOSS IN MULTIPLE BIRTH
(CLIMB, INC.)
P.O. Box 91377
Anchorage, AK 99509
Tel: (907) 222-5321
www.climb-support.org

CENTER FOR LOSS AND RENEWAL
168 West 86th Street, Suite 1D
New York, NY 10024
Tel: (212) 874-4711
Fax: (212) 749-2481

THE COMPASSIONATE FRIENDS, INC.
P.O. Box 3696
Oak Brook, IL 60522-3696
Tel: (708) 990-0010
Fax: (630) 990-0246
Toll free: (877) 969-0010
www.compassionatefriends.org

HAND—HELPING AFTER NEONATAL
DEATH
P.O. Box 341
Los Gatos, CA 95031
Tel: (800) 963-7070
www.h-a-n-d.org

HOPING—HELPING OTHER PARENTS
IN NORMAL GRIEVING
Sparrow Hospital
1215 East Michigan Avenue
P.O. Box 30480
Lansing, MI 48090-9986
Tel: (517) 484-3873

HOSPICE OF THE CHESAPEAKE
8424 Veterans Highway
Millersville, MD 21108
Tel: (410) 987-2003
Fax: (410) 987-3961

IN LOVING MEMORY
1416 Green Run Lake
Reston, VA 22090
Tel: (703) 435-0608

M.E.N.D.—MOMMIES ENDURING
NEONATAL DEATH
P.O. Box 1007
Coppell, TX 75019
Tel:(888) 695-6363
www.mend.org

MISCARRIAGE, INFANT DEATH AND
STILLBIRTH (MIDS) INC.
16 Crescent Drive
Parsippany, NJ 07054

MOTHERS IN SYMPATHY AND SUPPORT
(MISS)
P.O. Box 5333
Peoria, AZ 85385-53333
Tel: (623) 979-1000

NATIONAL CENTER FOR THE
PREVENTION OF SUDDEN INFANT
DEATH SYNDROME
330 West Charles Street
Baltimore, MD 21201
Tel: (800) 547-SIDS

NATIONAL HOSPICE ORGANIZATION
(NHO)
1901 North Moore Street, Suite 901
Arlington, VA 22209
Tel: (800) 658-8898
Fax: (710) 525-5762

NATIONAL SUDDEN INFANT DEATH
SYNDROME FOUNDATION
2 Metro Plaza, Suite 205
8240 Professional Place
Landover, MD 20785

PREGNANCY AND INFANT LOSS CENTER
1421 E. Wayzata Boulevard, #40
Wayzata, MN 55391
Tel: (612) 473-9372

RESOLVE THROUGH SHARING
BEREAVEMENT SERVICES
Gunderson/Lutheran Medical Center
1910 South Avenue
La Crosse, WI 54601
Tel: (800) 362-9567

ROBERTSON BEREAVEMENT CENTER
797 North Court Street
Medina, OH 44256
Tel: (330) 725-1900
Toll free: (800) 700-4771
www.ohio.net

ROBERT H. WAHLS BEREAVEMENT
CENTER
30 Broadway
Kingston, NY 12401
Tel: 338-2273
Fax: 338-7321

SHARE—PREGNANCY AND INFANT
LOSS SUPPORT, INC.
St. Joseph Health Center
300 First Capitol Drive
St. Charles, MO 63301-2893
Tel: (314) 947-5000
Toll free: (800) 821-6819
www.nationalSHAREoffice.com

SIDS ALLIANCE
10500 Little Patuxent Parkway
Columbia, MD 21044
Tel: (800) 221-SIDS

ST. VINCENT HOSPITALS AND HEALTH
SERVICES
2001 West 86th Street
Indianapolis, IN 46240
Tel: (317) 338-2273
Toll-free: (888) 338-2273

THE STURBRIDGE GROUP
Bereavement Training and
Consultation
249 Ayer Road, Suite 204
Harvard, MA 01451
Tel: (508) 653-1609
www.sturbridgegroup.com

TENDER HEARTS GROUP
1382 Aralia Court
San Luis Obispo, CA 93401
Tel: (805) 545-0617

TWINLESS TWIN SUPPORT—ITA
11220 St. Joe Road
Fort Wayne, IN 46835
Tel: (219) 627-5414

UNICORN BEREAVEMENT CENTER
Triangle Hospice at The
Meadowlands
1001 Corporate Drive
Hillsborough, NC 27278
Tel: (919) 644-6869
Fax: (919) 644-1541
www.trianglehospice.org

UNITE, INC.
Jeanes Hospital
7600 Central Avenue
Philadelphia, PA 19111-2499
Tel: (215) 728-3777

CANADA

BEREAVEMENT RESOURCE COUNCIL OF
ELGIN
400 Talbot Street
St. Thomas, ON N5P 1B8
Canada
Tel: (519) 633-2149
Toll-free: (800) 463-1810
www.elgin.net

GRIEF & LOSS RESOURCE CENTRE
Box 1290
Golden, BC V0A 1H0
Canada

HELPING OTHER PARENTS ENDURE
(HOPE)
4833 Straume Avenue
Terrace, BC V8G 2C8
Canada

SHATTERED DREAMS (MISCARRIAGE)
21 Potsdam Road
Unit 61
Downsview, Ontario M3N 1N3
Canada
Tel: (416) 663-7142

List of
Further Reading

HE FOLLOWING IS A LIST OF THOSE BOOKS I HAVE found most accessible. You should check with your local library for additional titles.

Allen, Marie, and Shelley Marks. *Miscarriage: Women Sharing from the Heart.* New York: John Wiley & Sons, 1993.

Jones, Wendy. *Miscarriage: Overcoming the Physical and Emotional Trauma.* New York: Harper Collins, 1990.

McKissock, Mal. *Coping with Grief.* Sydney: ABC Books, 1985.

Nichol, Margaret. *Loss of a Baby, Death of a Dream: Understanding Maternal Grief.* Sydney: HarperCollins, 1997.

Overs, Marge. *Coping with Miscarriage.* Sydney: Gore and Osment, 1995.

Plater, Diana. *Taking Control: How to Aim for a Successful Pregnancy after Miscarriage, Stillbirth or Neonatal Loss.* Sydney: Transworld, 1997.

Acknowledgments

HERE ARE MANY PEOPLE WITHOUT WHOM THIS BOOK would not have been written, and I shall be eternally grateful to them all. Sue Williams encouraged me to do more than just dream, started the ball rolling, and introduced me to my wonderful agent, Selwa Anthony. Both of these incredible women supported and encouraged me throughout the emotional roller coaster that was to be my first journey into writing. I'm proud to call you friends.

Julie Gibbs, my publisher, believed in the book even before it was written, and Meredith Rose, my editor, was there for me with her gentle assistance and advice. My special thanks to you both.

Professor Michael J. Bennett, head of the school of obstetrics and gynecology at the Royal Hospital for Women in Sydney, Australia, responded to my call for help and frequently found time in his busy schedule to answer my questions. Moreover, he gave me the rare opportunity to speak with other medical professionals from a parent's perspective. Thank you.

My husband, Peter, and our daughters, Elizabeth and Georgina, had to live with me and still love me, no matter how difficult I became and how unreasonable I was during the months I spent researching and writing. I love you so very much.

It is the women and men who wrote to me, however, to whom I am most grateful. They have all shown extraordinary courage and strength in coming forward and revisiting their pain. Without them the silence would remain. These are our stories.

Little Angels

I know God has room for just two more Angels
Two Angels who float on top of my heart alone
And those two Angels are Simon and Clare

Simon and Clare
Those names ring in my head like church bells

If I could take Mum's place then perhaps I would understand
How two simple people have changed her life forever.

(BY GEORGINA RYAN, 1999)